Mel Bay Presents

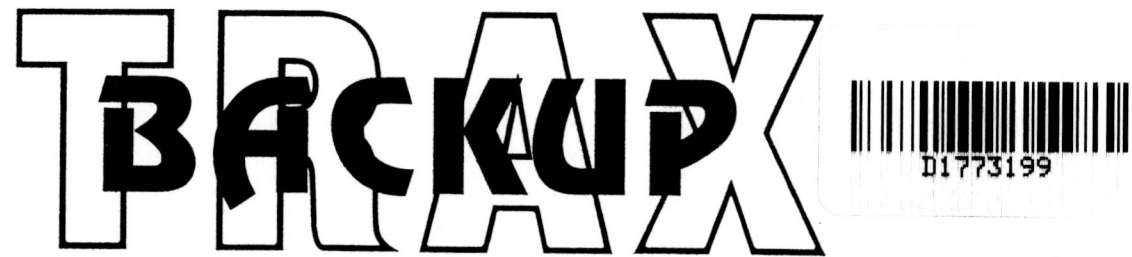

Swing & Jazz Vol. 1

For: Guitar, Violin, Mandolin, Banjo, Flute and Other C Instruments

Guitar and Mandolin Tablature Included

Book/CD Play-Along!

Learn melodies and practice soloing on twelve of the most popular and important chord progressions in the swing and jazz repertoire — cycle of fifths, major and minor progressions with two-five-one, one-six-two-five-one, one-three-six-two-five chord changes, major, minor and 6/8 blues and much more — all based on your favorite swing and jazz hits. Play along with a hot rhythm section: guitar, mandolin, and bass; etude melodies played on tenor sax — excellent for reed and horn players. The compact disc has all of the tunes at slow and regular speeds with melodies, and allows you to hear just rhythm, just lead, or both. **We'll play all night long!**

by Dix Bruce

CD CONTENTS

1. Introduction (:32)
2. Tuning (:32)
3. Cycles Slow (1:32)
4. Cycles licks (:27)
5. Cycles band (4:05)
6. Hollyhock Tulip slow (1:45)
7. Hollyhock Tulip licks (:25)
8. Hollyhock Tulip band (4:41)
9. Blues in G slow (:56)
10. Blues in G licks (:23)
11. Blues in G band (2:57)
12. Slow Rhythm (1:36)
13. Slow Rhythm licks (:26)
14. Slow Rhythm band (5:03)
15. Michigan slow (2:14)
16. Michigan licks (:24)
17. Michigan band (5:21)
18. Fast Rhythm (4:08)
19. Fast Blues slow (:37)
20. Fast Blues licks (:31)
21. Fast Blues band (2:48)
22. Gal Be Bad slow (1:48)
23. Gal Be Bad licks (:29)
24. Gal Be Bad band (4:59)
25. Blues in C Minor slow (:24)
26. Blues in C Minor licks (:20)
27. Blues in C Minor band (2:39)
28. Solo in Sun slow (1:27)
29. Solo in Sun lick (:33)
30. Solo in Sun lick (:20)
31. Solo in Sun band (3:29)
32. 6/8 Blues slow (1:08)
33. 6/8 Blues lick (:17)
34. 6/8 Blues band (2:51)
35. Yellowstone slow (1:41)
36. Yellowstone lick (:21)
37. Yellowstone band (4:52)
38. Closing (1:27)

1 2 3 4 5 6 7 8 9 0

© 1992 BY MEL BAY PUBLICATIONS, INC., PACIFIC, MO 63069.
ALL RIGHTS RESERVED. INTERNATIONAL COPYRIGHT SECURED. B.M.I. MADE AND PRINTED IN U.S.A.

Visit us on the Web at http://www.melbay.com — E-mail us at email@melbay.com

CONTENTS

Foreword to *BackUp Trax* 3
Introduction to *Swing & Jazz* 4
Cycles 8
Hollyhock Tulip 11
Blues in G 14
Slow Rhythm 17
Michigan 20
Fast Rhythm 23
Fast Blues 24
Gal Be Bad 27
Blues in C Minor 30
Solo the Sun 33
6/8 Blues 39
Yellowstone 42

Dix Bruce is a musician, writer and award-winning guitar player from the San Francisco Bay Area. He edited ***Mandolin World News*** from 1978 to 1984 and has recorded two albums with bluegrass legend Frank Wakefield. He recently completed a solo folk recording, *My Folk Heart,* and has just released a band recording of string swing & jazz, *Tuxedo Blues,* with many of his original compositions. He is a columnist for the Fretted Instrument Guild of America newsletter, was a frequent contributor to ***FRETS*** magazine, and writes for ***Acoustic Guitar.*** He has taught mandolin, guitar, and bass for nearly 20 years. He also tours and records with The Royal Society Jazz Orchestra, a big band from San Francisco.

FOREWORD TO *BACKUP TRAX*

When I was first learning to play leads on the guitar and mandolin, an older and wiser musician friend suggested that I practice with taped rhythm sections. That way I could hear the chords, practice playing over them in the context of the song's form, and repeat whatever I was working on until I'd perfected it. It was almost as good as playing with a live band and offered the opportunity of infinite repetition as I honed this lick or that solo. For the past fifteen years I have included rhythm-track playing in my daily practice routine.

To say that it helped me enormously would be an understatement. It improved my timing and rhythm playing. My melodies and solos got better, cleaner, and more focused as I practiced solos or licks hundreds of times. I owe a great deal of my playing ability to this type of practicing. These days I often use two tape machines, the first to play the rhythm track and the second to record my playing to the track. (Of course, if you have a multi-track recorder you can do it with one machine.) This really lets you know how well you are playing.

Because of my positive experiences with practice recordings, I've always encouraged my students to make and use their own. Unfortunately I've found that some students are not developmentally ready to provide themselves with good grooves and tempos. Since there were no string rhythm tracks available on the market, I decided to round up some of the best rhythm players in the San Francisco Bay Area and put them on a recording. *BackUp Trax* is the result.

The purpose of *BackUp Trax* is to give musicians a rhythm section to play along with and rehearse melodies, solos, licks, and rhythm playing. *BackUp Trax* offers the advantage of infinite repetition; you can work on a tune, solo, or passage for hours, perfecting it without wearing out your fellow players. The opportunities for advancing your reading and improvising skills while expanding your repertoire are unlimited.

Each *BackUp Trax* set comes with a compact disc and a book of chord charts, melodies (in both standard notation and tablature), and playing tips. Melodies to each of the tunes are recorded at about one-half speed with just guitar accompaniment before each track with the full band. Instruments are isolated and panned for maximum flexibility. By adjusting the balance control on your stereo amplifier you can hear 1) the full band of guitar, mandolin, bass and melody lead in stereo (played on fiddle on the *Old Time & Fiddle Tunes* edition and on guitar on the *Swing & Jazz* edition), 2) just guitar and bass, or 3) just mandolin, melody, and bass. Tones for tuning are at the beginning of each recording.

Have fun, good luck, and happy playing!

INTRODUCTION TO *SWING & JAZZ*

Welcome to the *Swing & Jazz* edition of *BackUp Trax*. It includes eleven pieces, twelve tracks, carefully chosen to represent a variety of keys and types of tunes encountered in the swing & jazz repertoire. You'll play fast and slow blues, minor blues, "rhythm changes" tunes, ballads, cycle of fifths, "ii-V-I" tunes and more. These same progressions recur again and again in pop, swing, and jazz. By learning to play melodies and solo over them in this generic form you'll give yourself a great head start toward becoming a swing & jazz player. You can also use these melodies as solos on similar standard tunes.

Melodies and chord progressions to all the tunes in this book are on the recording at regular and slow speeds. Tuning tones are at the beginning of the recording.

Here are some tips for working with the *Swing & Jazz BackUp Trax:*

1) **Familiarize** yourself with the melodies and chord progressions by listening and reading before you play along.

2) **Try** from the very beginning to relate these changes to popular standards. Consult original sheet music or fake books for ideas. Look for overall similarities in form and chord progression; then, most importantly, identify common chord passages that occur again and again. This will take some study but you'll end up using these "chunks" as building blocks for understanding unfamiliar tunes and playing over their changes.

For example, the 1-measure ii-V change in "Hollyhock Tulip" is *everywhere* in the repertoire. When you find it in another tune, you can lift fragments of the "Hollyhock" melody or licks and plug them into the new tune. This will work in any tune with the ii-V change, in any key!

[Don't be confused by different keys or transposing. Try to look at the chord changes in the context of the tune's home key. Identify the chords numerically — I, ii, iii, IV, V, vi, vii, etc. (lower-case numerals denote minor chords) — rather than alphabetically — G, Am, Bm, C, D, Em, F♯°, etc. That way you'll see that a ii chord (Am) in the key of G functions exactly like a ii (B♭m) in the key of A♭ and that you can play the same thing, transposed up one-half step, over both.]

Another example is the III-VI-II-V progression in the bridge to "Rhythm." This is another of the basic pop building blocks. You can lift individual dominant seven licks (for chords like D7, G7, C7, etc.), or use several-measure dominant seven phrases anywhere similar chord changes occur.

This type of practice will help you build a kind of generic approach to playing the swing & jazz repertoire. You can then look at any new tune as a combination of parts, for example, "ii-V-I in G followed by ii-V-i in A minor, then a III-VI-II-V bridge." The understanding of individual parts will help you tackle the whole.

3) Once you've familiarized yourself with the tunes, memorize the given melodies while playing along with the slow version of the piece. Gradually work your way up to the regular speed.

4) Next try plugging melodies from well-known standards into the recorded format. Take an entire melody of a similar standard and fit it into the given recorded example. Try also to isolate and apply 2-, 4-, 8-, or 16-measure phrases over the given changes. Again use the slow version with the melody turned off. This, along with the suggestions below, will help you build a vocabulary of several-bar phrases.

5) Now try making up your own solos. Start by isolating phrases, thinking of them generically as to how they fit over changes. Use the licks given. Transpose, modify, change and recycle them to include your own ideas. Be sure to practice playing the licks on other tunes and in other keys. All you have to do is look for matching chord changes and plug them in. Be sure to make up your own licks. Don't be afraid to quote the melody. The slow versions of the tunes can help you formulate your solos at a relaxed speed. Transitions between phrases needs to flow and naturally connect.

6) At jam sessions, substitute the melodies you've learned for composed melodies on similar standards. This is probably the most important exercise you'll do in that it will bridge the gap between the tunes on the recording and tunes you'll encounter on the gig. Here is where you make the generic approach pay off, but you have to take the time to identify similarities and plug in appropriate melodic fragments. The melodies you've learned can be used as solos, in whole or part. Use chunks of these melodies and fill in the rest with your own ideas.

7) Finally, don't forget to practice playing rhythm along with us, even if you don't play a chordal instrument. Make up your own rhythm riffs and work them. A good rhythmic sense is probably the most important component of good musicianship. It's really true that "it don't mean a thing if it ain't got that swing."

You'll notice that all the music is presented in four versions/keys: concert C for string, keyboard, or any other concert-pitched instrument; B♭ for trumpet, clarinet, tenor and soprano sax or any other B♭ instrument; E♭ for baritone and alto sax, or any other E♭ instrument; and bass clef for trombone, etc. Just about any instrumentalist can play along with the recording by choosing the correct version for his or her instrument.

Dix Bruce — Guitar
Photo by Rob Thomas

You can also use the versions *not* in your key to help you practice transposing. Transposing is a necessity if you play with others, especially singers. A male voice might typically sing a song in F, while a female voice might sing the same song in B♭ or C. You have to be able to adapt. Transposition is not a terribly difficult thing to do, it just takes a little practice. Start by playing the tunes in the two other keys. Remember: You won't be able to play along with the recording in these new keys, and you'll have to change the chords your accompanist uses.

Guitar and mandolin tablature are also included.

The best general advice I can offer is to listen and play. Simple as that. It's very important that you hear what other players, live and on record, do with these changes. Don't just listen to players of your particular instrument; check out pianists, string players, percussionists, horn players, etc. Make yourself curious enough to listen to your favorite recorded musicians play a lick or passage until you figure it out — a hundred times if necessary. Learn to sing what you're trying to play, even if you have a lousy voice. Look for new ideas and input constantly, and try to make them a part of your playing. Most of all, remember that music is supposed to be fun, for both players and listeners. When it ain't fun, something's wrong! So, have fun above all else!

The players on the recording are Bob Alekno, mandolin; Mike Wollenberg, bass; and myself, Dix Bruce, guitar. Bob is an excellent source of rhythm licks. Special thanks to Keith Baumann and David Grisman for their generous help with Macintosh technology, to Nick Phelps for his help with the horn version of the tunes, and to Bill DeKuiper and Valerie Sopher for their valuable suggestions.

If you have any comments, suggestions, or questions about *BackUp Trax*, please drop me a line c/o MUSIX, P.O. Box 231005, Pleasant Hill, CA 94523. Let's play all night long!

— Dix Bruce

Mike Wollenberg — Bass
Bob Alekno — Mandolin
Photo by Dave Gilbert

SPECIAL NOTE ABOUT THE TABLATURE

Most of the chord diagrams shown with the tablature are in closed and thus moveable positions. The "R" below a chord grid shows which string the chord's root tone is played on. "X"s denote strings that should be muted with the fretting hand and not played. Chords with open strings are not moveable. The small boxed fret number to the right of the grid shows where the chord is played.

Some chords, like the G7 mandolin chord in "Cycles," don't include a root. In these cases the seventh or another part of the chord is noted. In others, like the B♭ mandolin chord in "Rhythm" or the G guitar chord in "Gal Be Bad," you'll find two or three roots.

Most of the guitar chords use four strings, most of the mandolin chords use three. In some cases different positions are shown with the same chord name. This was done to minimize hand movement up and down the neck and to familiarize you with other possible chord choices. Be sure to experiment with alternate chord positions as well as chord substitutions. For more information see Mel Bay's *Rhythm Guitar Chord System* (MB93214), *Jazz Guitar Method* by Ronnie Lee (MB93240), or any good jazz chord method book.

CYCLES

Similar to tunes like "Sweet Georgia Brown," "Don't Let Your Deal Go Down," and the bridge to "I've Got Rhythm," "Cycles'" chords move mostly in a VI-II-V-I pattern. Find one dominant 7 lick and use it over each of the dominant 7 chords by transposing it from D7 to G7 to C7, etc. The last 8 bars throw a slight curve with the Dm-to-A7 change (six minor to three dominant). Experiment until you find something that works. Start with chord arpeggios or scales. There's a suggestion below. Key of F.

© Copyright 1990 by Dix Bruce.

Cycles
Guitar Tablature

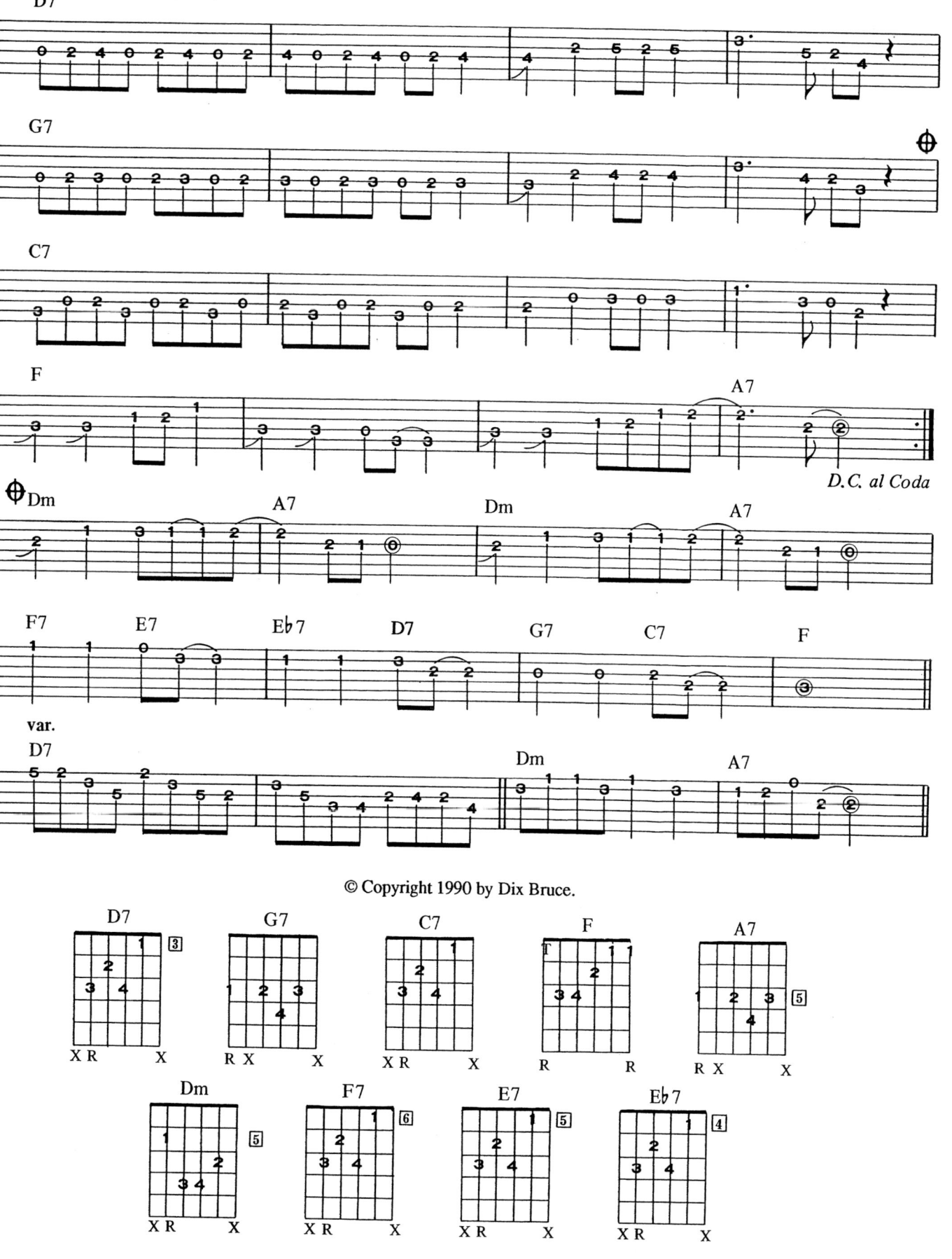

© Copyright 1990 by Dix Bruce.

Cycles
Mandolin Tablature

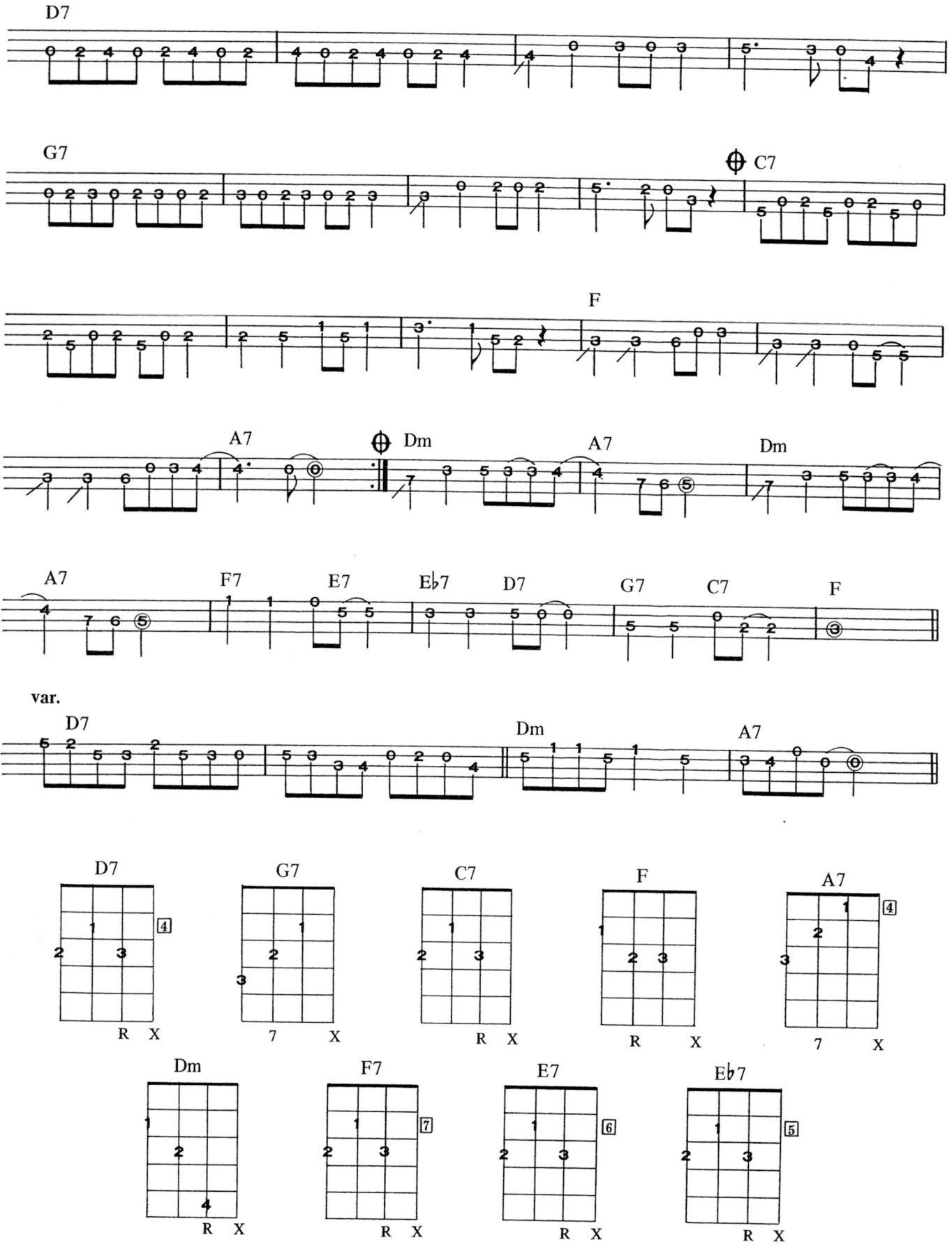

HOLLYHOCK TULIP

This tune, with its almost constant ii-V changes, is like a primer for pop music; ii-V is the most common move there is. In "Hollyhock" the changes come two per measure or one chord per two beats. In other tunes you'll find the ii-V change stretched to one chord per measure or one chord per four beats. While this change appears everywhere, the "Hollyhock Tulip" progression is most like tunes such as "Honeysuckle Rose" and "Scrapple from the Apple." Try substituting one 2-measure lick (I ii I V I) over spots where two 1-measure licks (I ii V I) are indicated. Notice the recurrence of the changes F-F#°-Gm7-C7 and F-F#°-Am7-Abm7. These are very typical "turnarounds" and lead you back to the I chord, in this case the F, or the top of the form. They can be used almost anywhere in place of 2 measures of a I chord or 1 measure each of the I and the V. The second lick shown is from the playing of Charlie Christian. Key of F.

© Copyright 1990 by Dix Bruce.

Hollyhock Tulip
Guitar Tablature

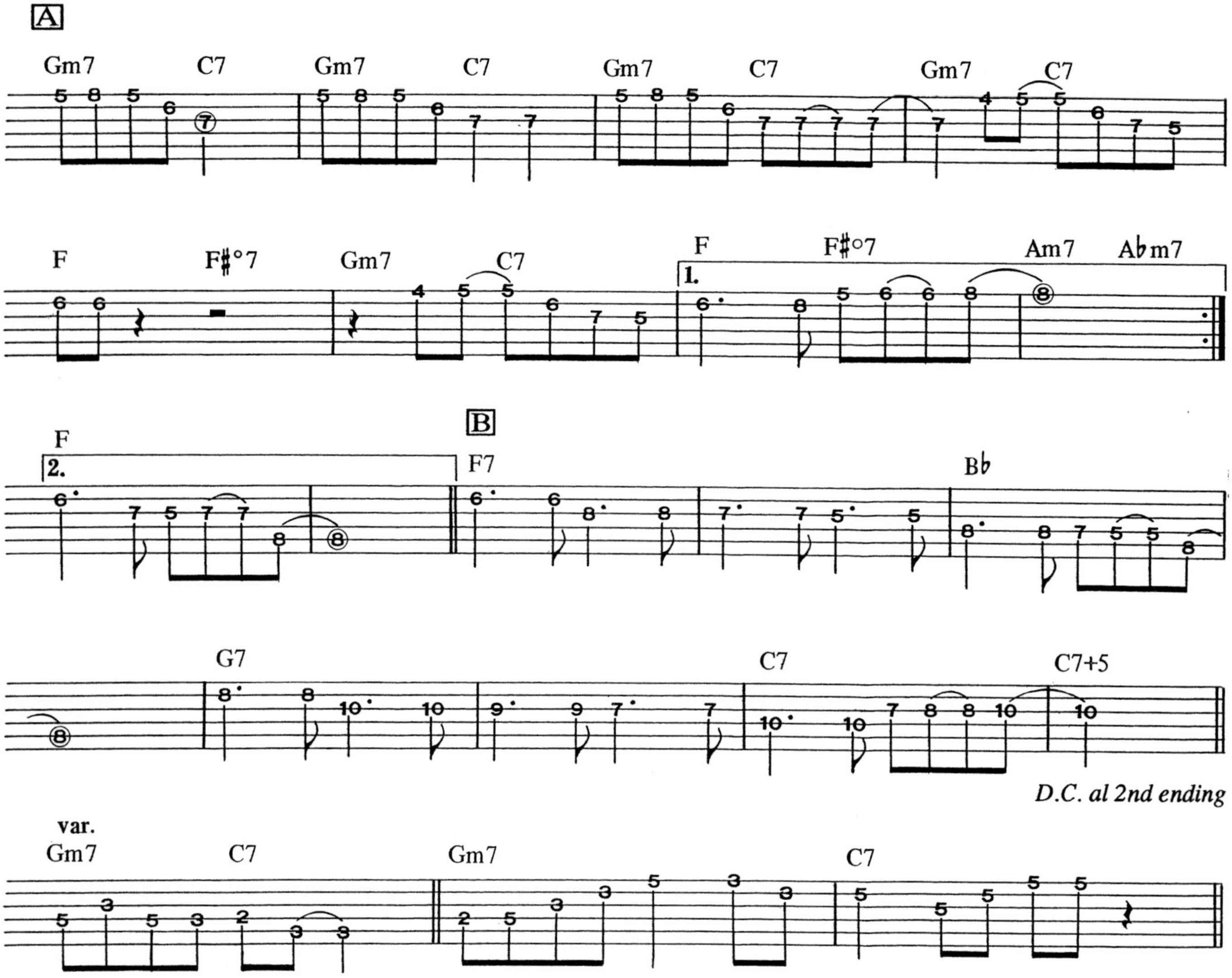

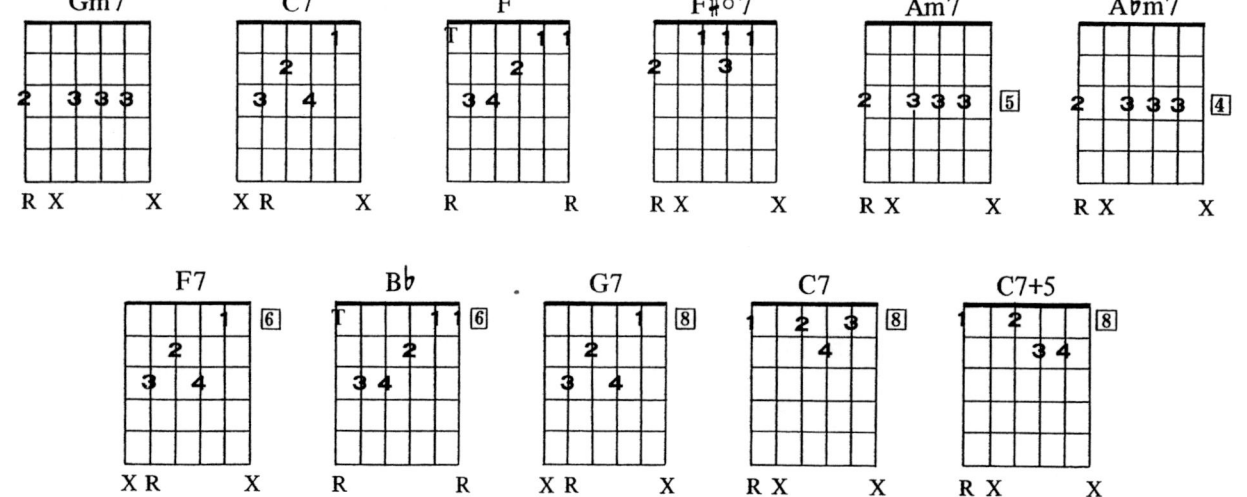

© Copyright 1990 by Dix Bruce.

Hollyhock Tulip
Mandolin Tablature

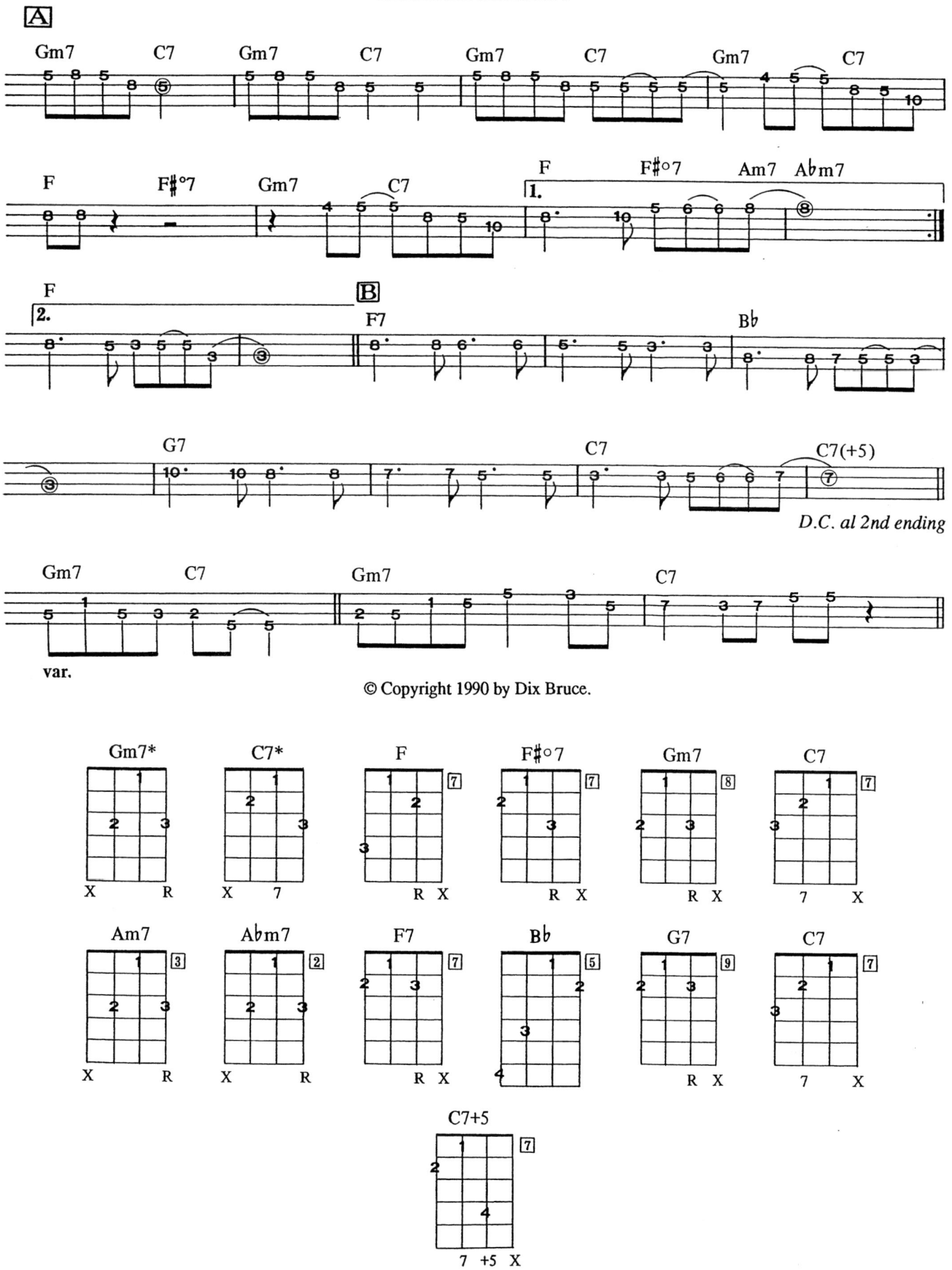

© Copyright 1990 by Dix Bruce.

*Note: You can also play these chords with the fourth string open — they just won't be moveable in that form.

BLUES IN G

What can one say about the blues? The blues is everywhere. It's a very common form in pop music. "Blues in G" is what's commonly known as a "riff blues." A riff blues is based on the repetition of one or two melodic phrases. Try making up your own riffs and melodies. Notice that "Blues in G" is written with two endings. Take the second only when you end the tune.

One thing the players on a recorded rhythm section can't do is react to your live playing. We can't follow your ideas or change to accommodate them. As such it's a bit artificial as a jam situation. You need input from and trading with other players. Not only will a good jamming group let you know when you're playing well, they'll also let you know when you're playing poorly! A jam session is also a great source of new material. Most importantly, it's a relaxed venue for learning to play with other people. You can't practice a thing like that by yourself. It's great to work with tapes or a metronome, but you need to take time to practice giving fellow players what they need to play their best. It's a subtle, evolving social skill that all group musicians must develop.

Jam whenever you can. I like small groups of three or four different instruments/people. With more than that I don't feel an exchange between players. It's always good to jam with musicians slightly better than you. It'll keep you working and learning. Key of G.

Blues in G
C Instruments

© Copyright 1990 by Dix Bruce.

Blues in G
Guitar Tablature

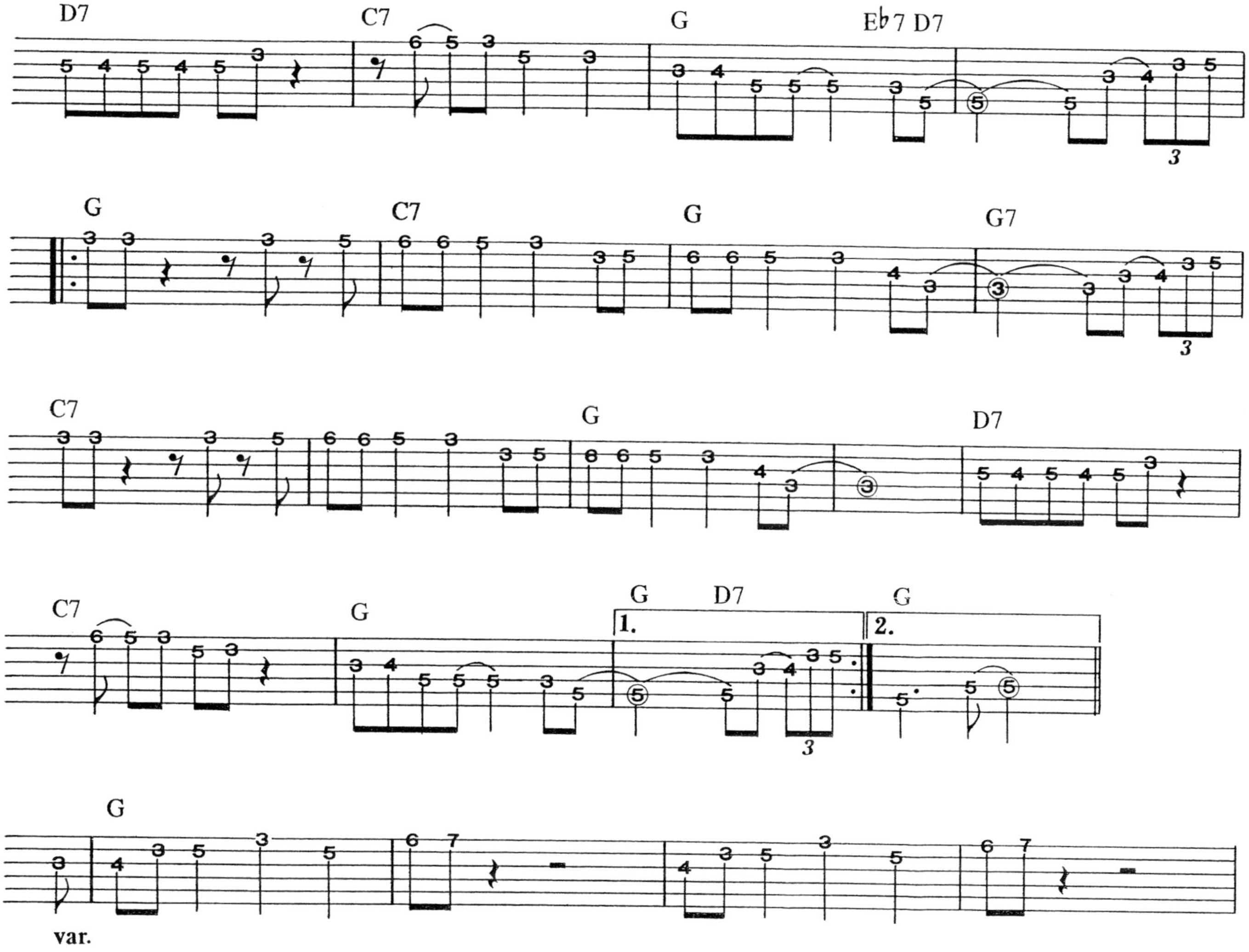

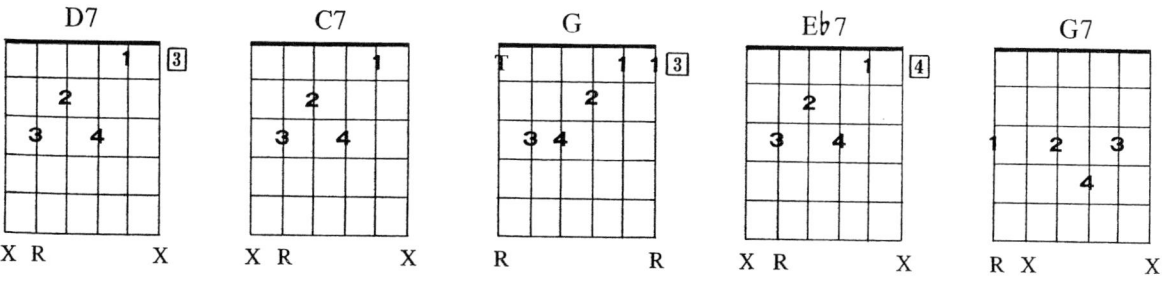

© Copyright 1990 by Dix Bruce.

Blues in G
Mandolin Tablature

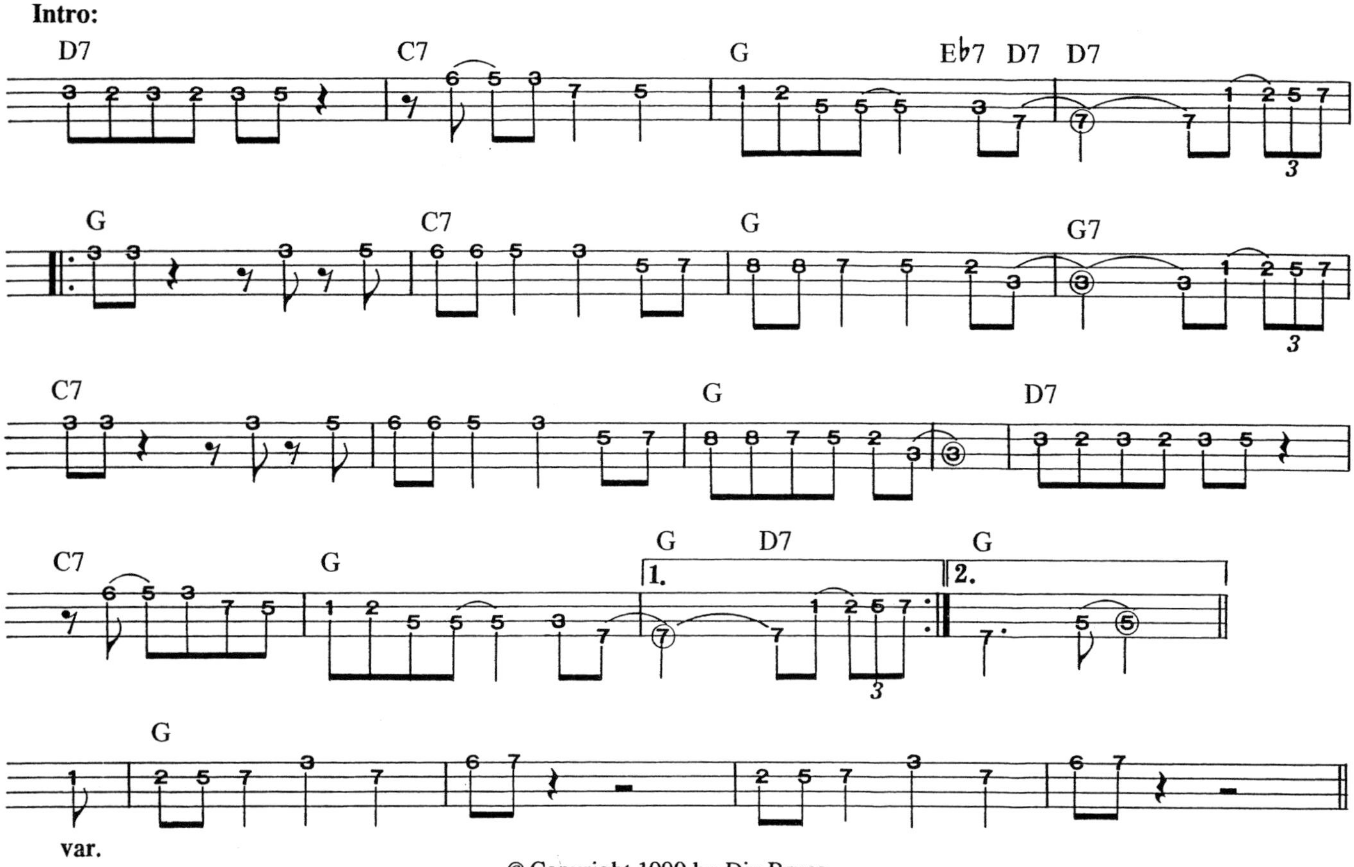

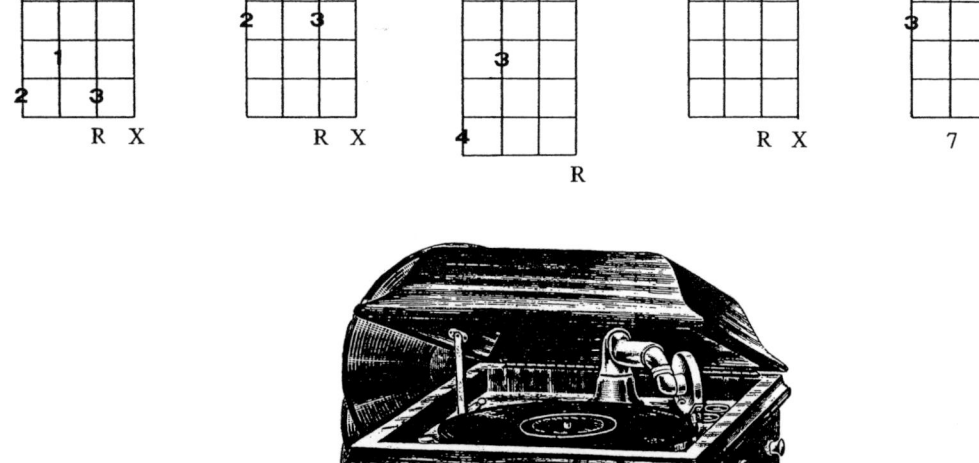

© Copyright 1990 by Dix Bruce.

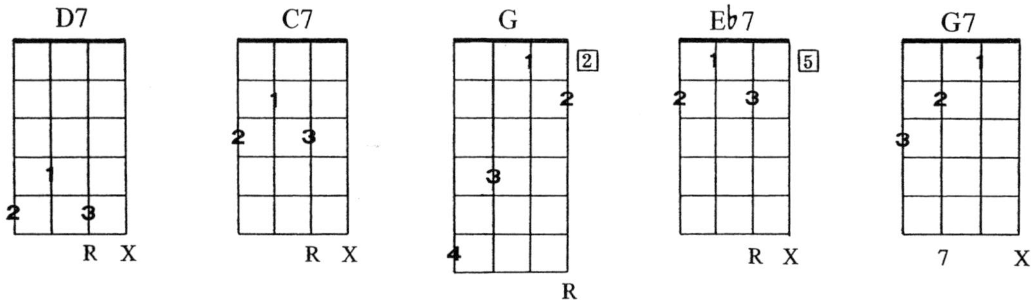

SLOW RHYTHM

You'll find hundreds of tunes based on what are called "rhythm changes." These include "I've Got Rhythm," Benny Goodman and Charlie Christian's "Seven Come Eleven," "The Flintstones Theme," George Benson's "Borgia Stick," Django and Stephane's "Swing 42," Charlie Parker's "Anthropology," and many more. Some of these so-called "rhythm" tunes include different bridges, extra measures, or slightly modified changes. |B♭ B°7|Cm7 F7| and |B♭ B°7|Cm7 C#°7| can be substituted for the given changes (|B♭ Gm7|Cm7 F7|). The changes to the second part of this tune, known as the bridge, are III-VI-II-V.

Since this tune is so prevalent and important in the pop and jazz repertoire, we've given you a slow and a fast full-band version to work with. Be sure to hit all of the changes. No cheating! Again, the second ending should be taken at the very end of the tune. If you've played the melody and are going to continue on with soloing, take the first ending as written or squeeze an F7 chord into the last two beats of the second ending. The F7, or V chord, will smoothly lead you back to the I or the beginning of the tune's form. If you get confused with any of the tunes' endings, check out the tape. Key of B♭.

Rhythm
C Instruments

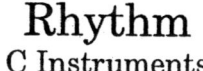

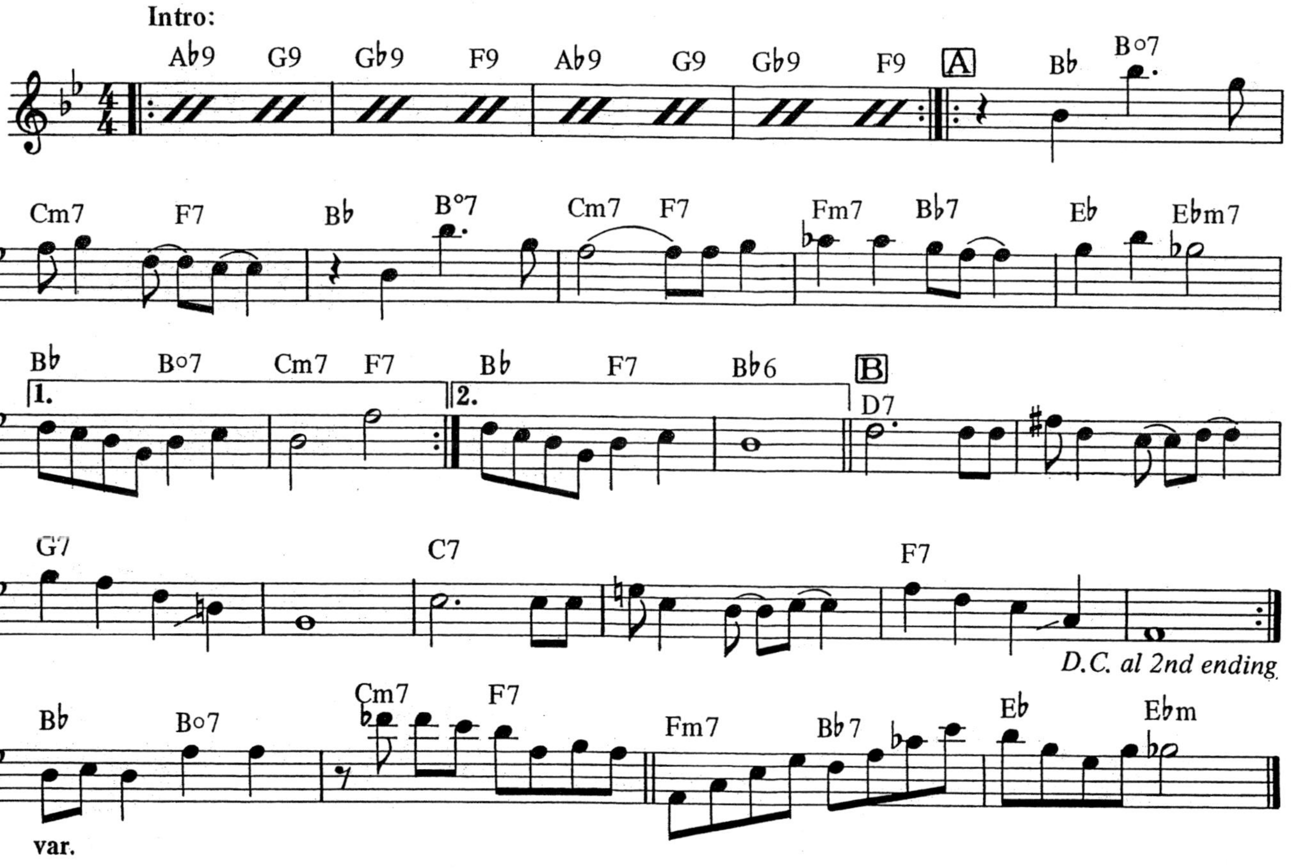

© Copyright 1990 by Dix Bruce.

Rhythm
Guitar Tablature

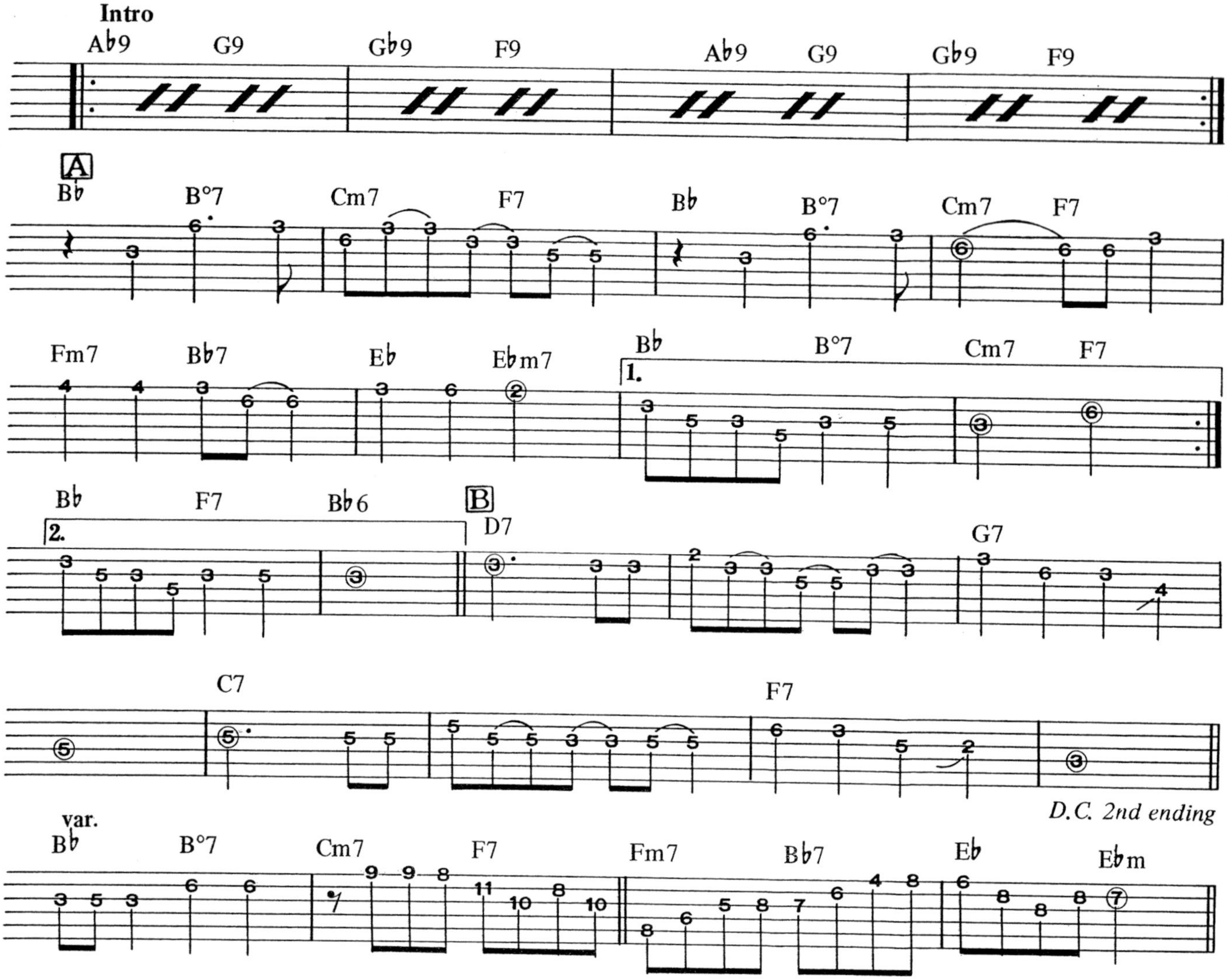

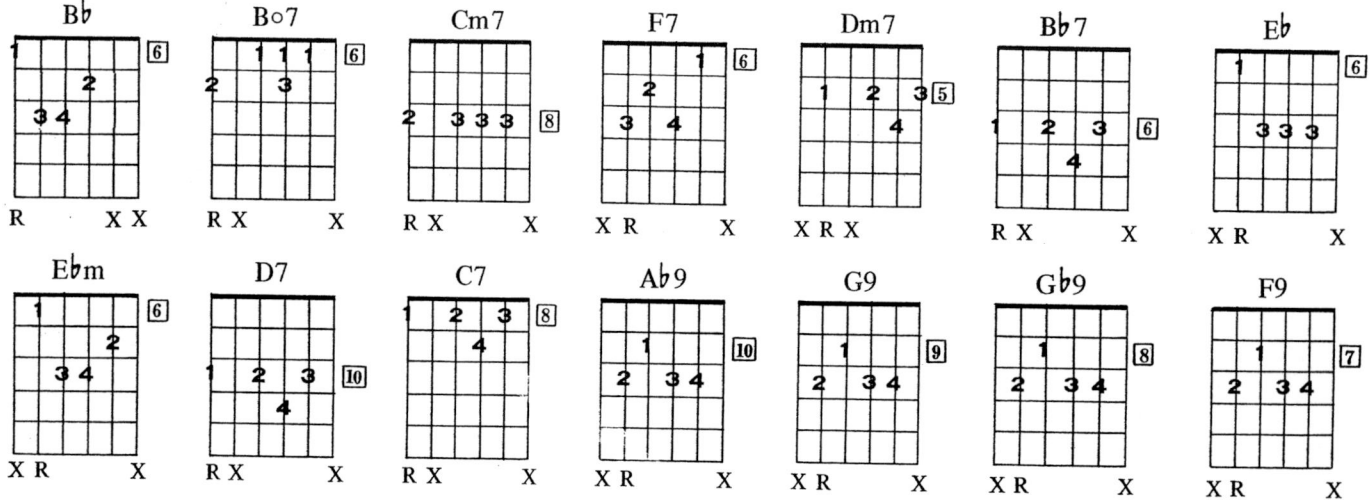

© Copyright 1990 by Dix Bruce.

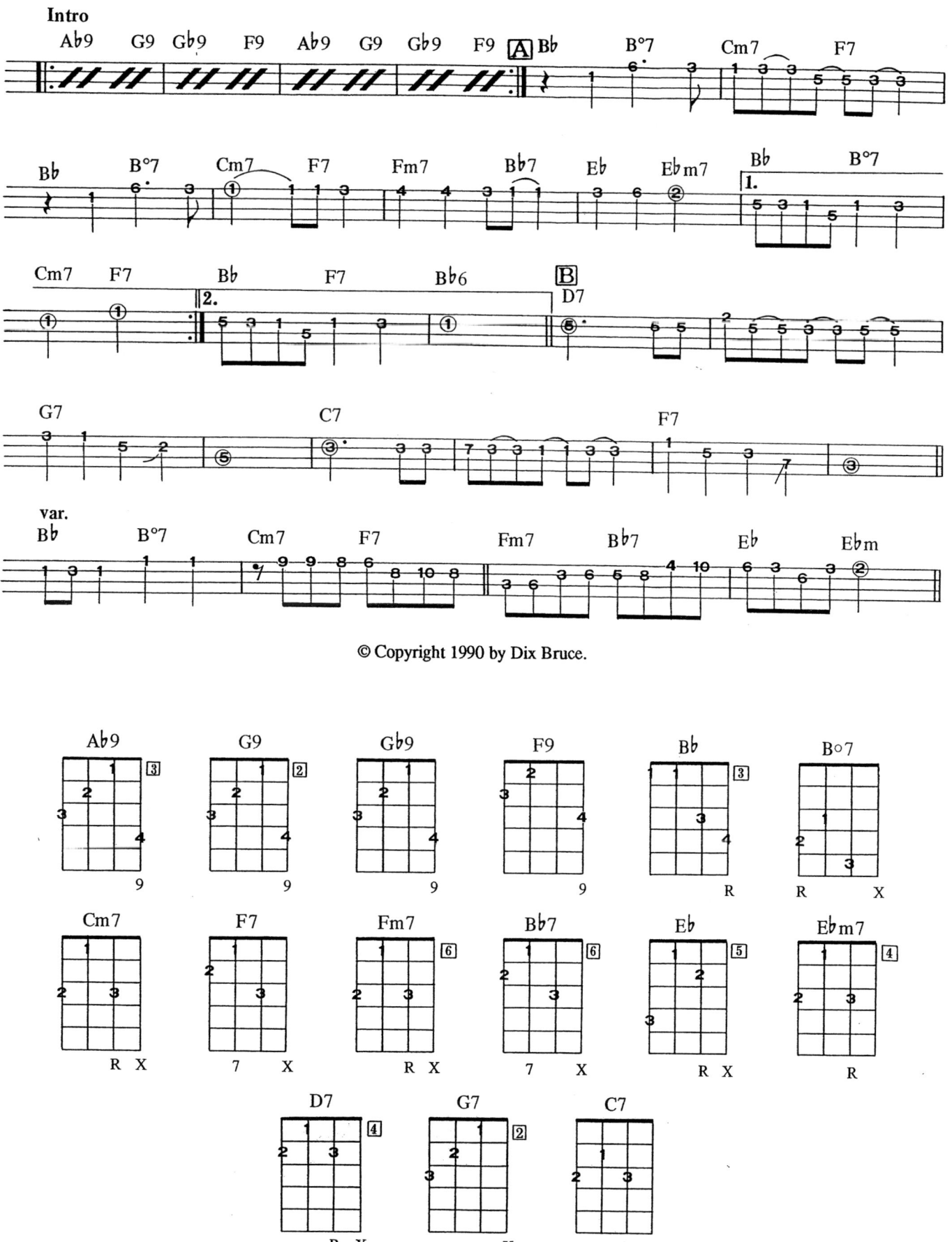

MICHIGAN

This ballad is similar to "Georgia" and has many of the chordal moves that we've already seen and some new ones, as well. The form is basically AABA, except that we use a *D.C. al Coda* to direct us to the third ending at the end of the piece. The final A part is nearly identical to the first except that, instead of using a turnaround like the first ending to take us back to the top, we're ending with 2 measures of F. Take the time to solo as melodically as you can. "Michigan" is great for practicing singing lines before you play them. Key of F.

Michigan
C Instruments

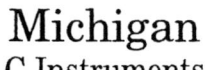

© Copyright 1990 by Dix Bruce.

Michigan
Guitar Tablature

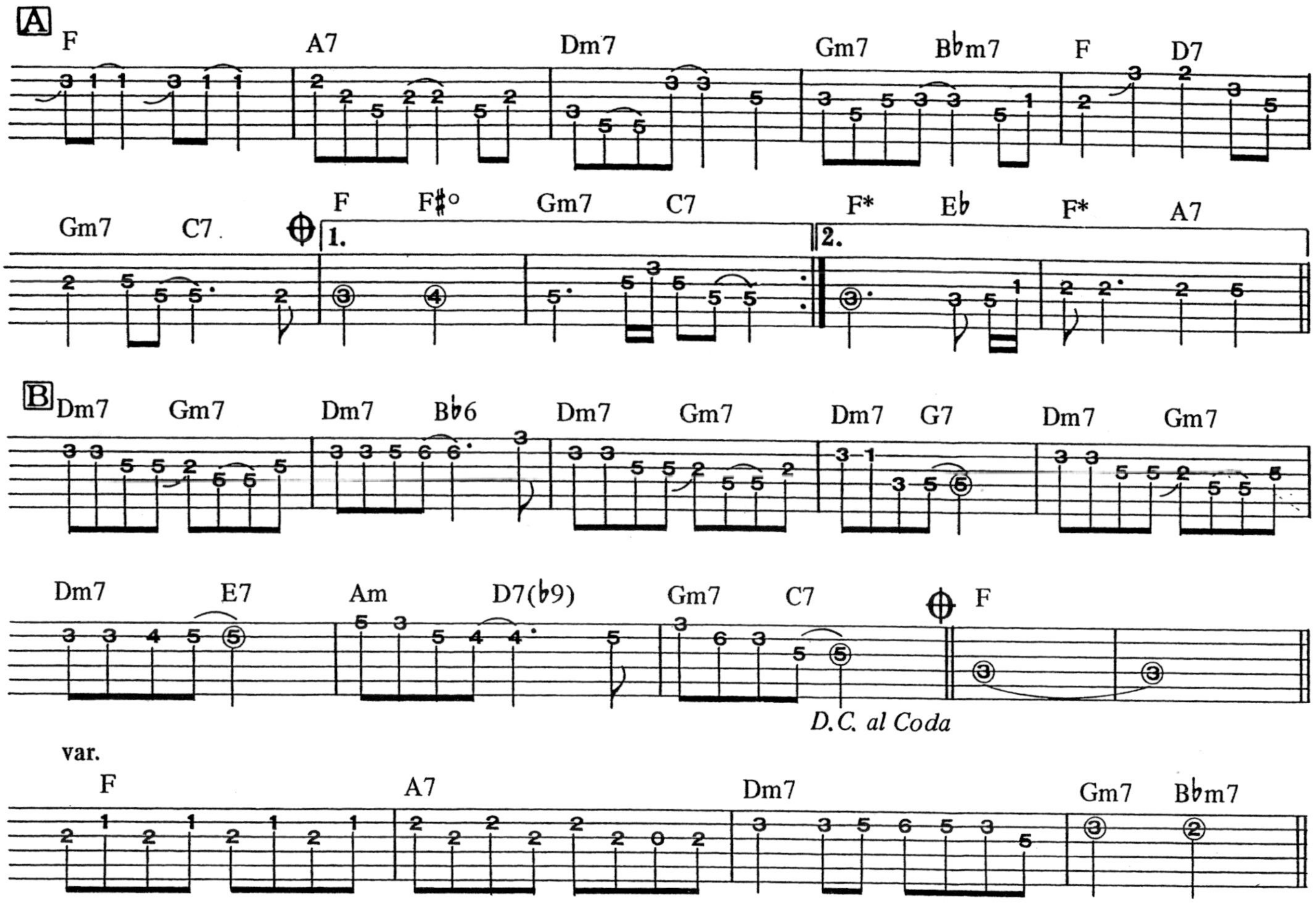

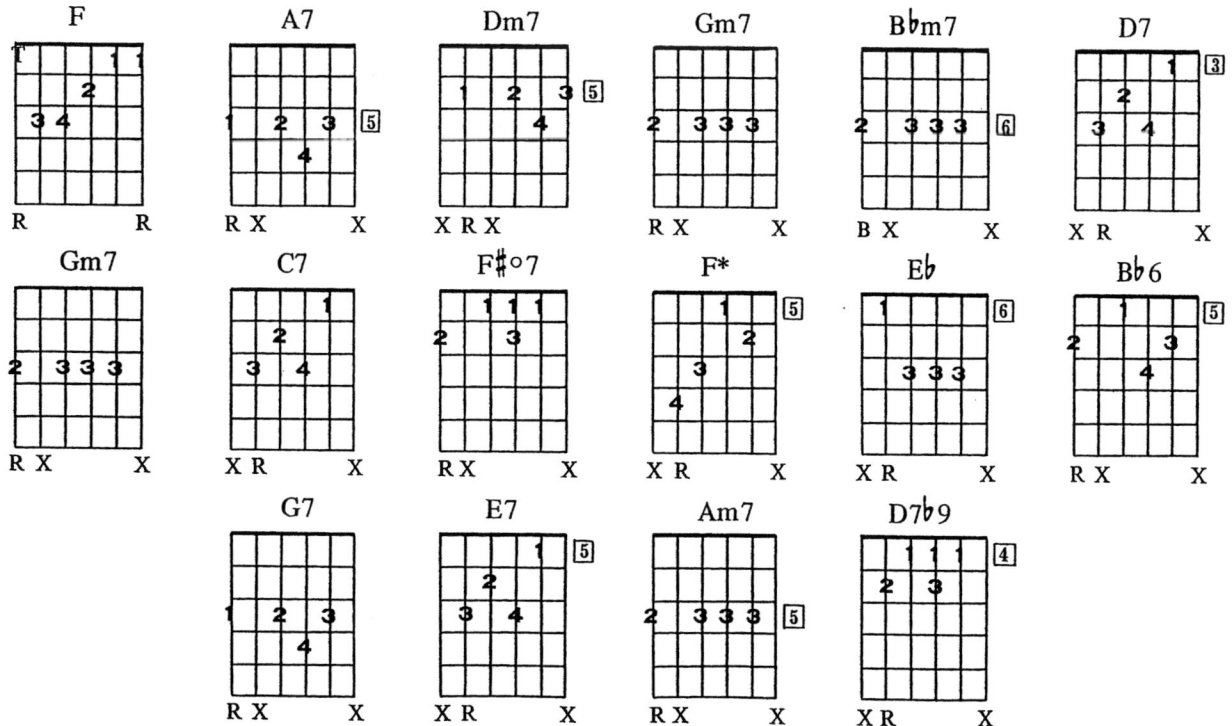

© Copyright 1990 by Dix Bruce.

Michigan
Mandolin Tablature

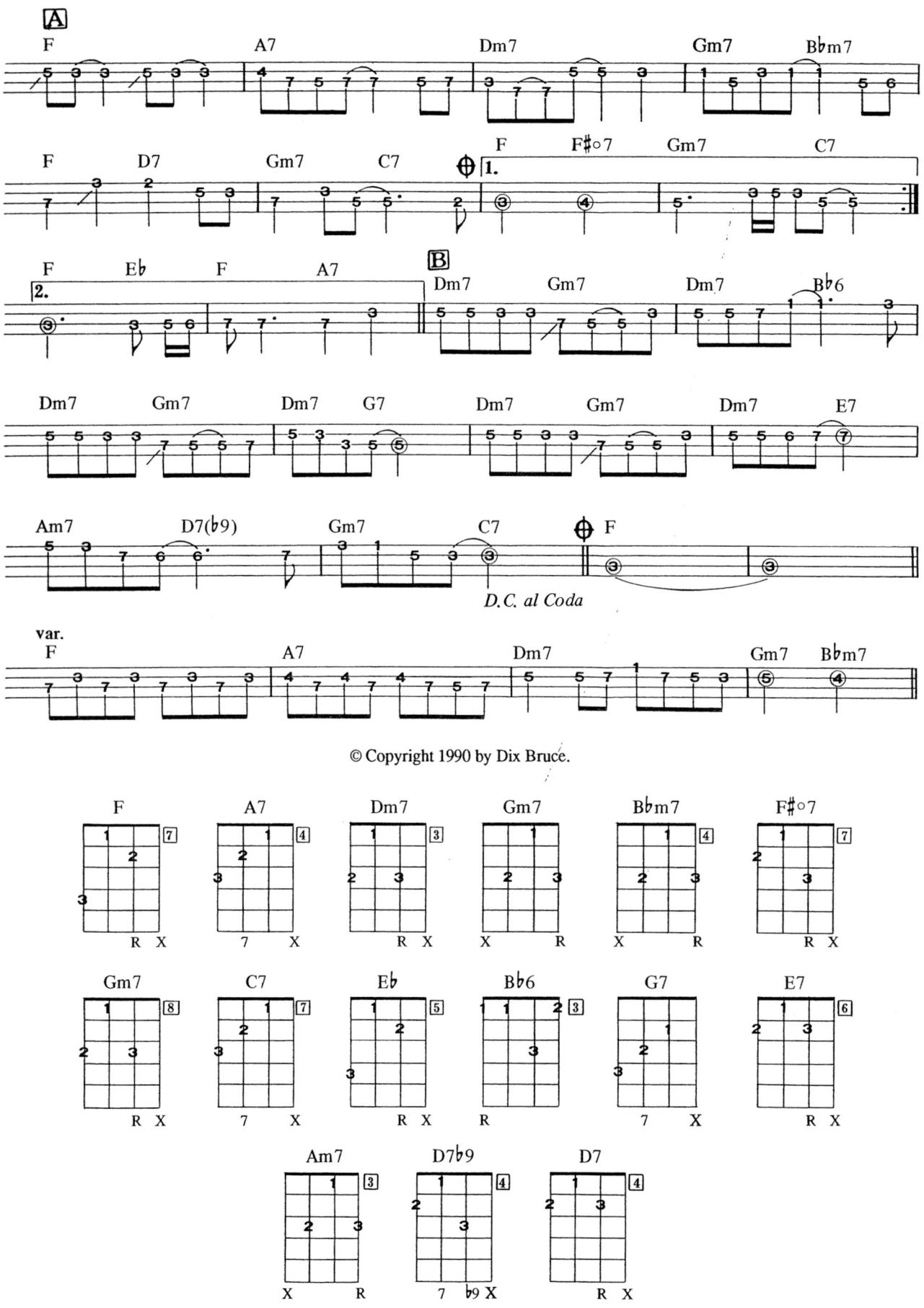

© Copyright 1990 by Dix Bruce.

FAST RHYTHM

Same as "Slow Rhythm," but guess what — faster! Don't forget to seek out other tunes with similar changes to each tune that you learn. You may be able to transfer only 2 or 4 bars, but that's the key to learning to solo in the swing & jazz repertoire. Train yourself to see the similarities and you'll never again be puzzled by a new tune. (Same music as "Slow Rhythm," page 16.) Key of B♭.

FAST BLUES

This is more jazz oriented than the previous blues and you'll notice that the changes are a bit more involved. As such, they'll give you different soloing possibilities than the simpler "G Blues." Check out the B♭°7/E♮°7 in the 6th measure leading back to the I. Notice also the ii-V-I passage beginning in the 9th measure and the turnaround beginning in the 11th measure. The second lick is one I heard mandolinist Tiny Moore play. Try transposing it to the key of G and using it in "Gal Be Bad."

As I mentioned in the introduction, you can utilize the other versions/keys (for reeds and horns) of any tune in this book. If you haven't already tried it, check out transposing "Fast Blues." All you have to do is read and learn the two charts that are *not* written for you. For example, if you are a guitar player, which is a concert C instrument, you can play "Fast Blues" in your key of B♭. If you read the B♭ instruments' chart you'll be in C, the E♭ chart will put you in G. Make sure you follow the appropriate chord changes. Key of B♭.

© Copyright 1990 by Dix Bruce.

Fast Blues
Guitar Tablature

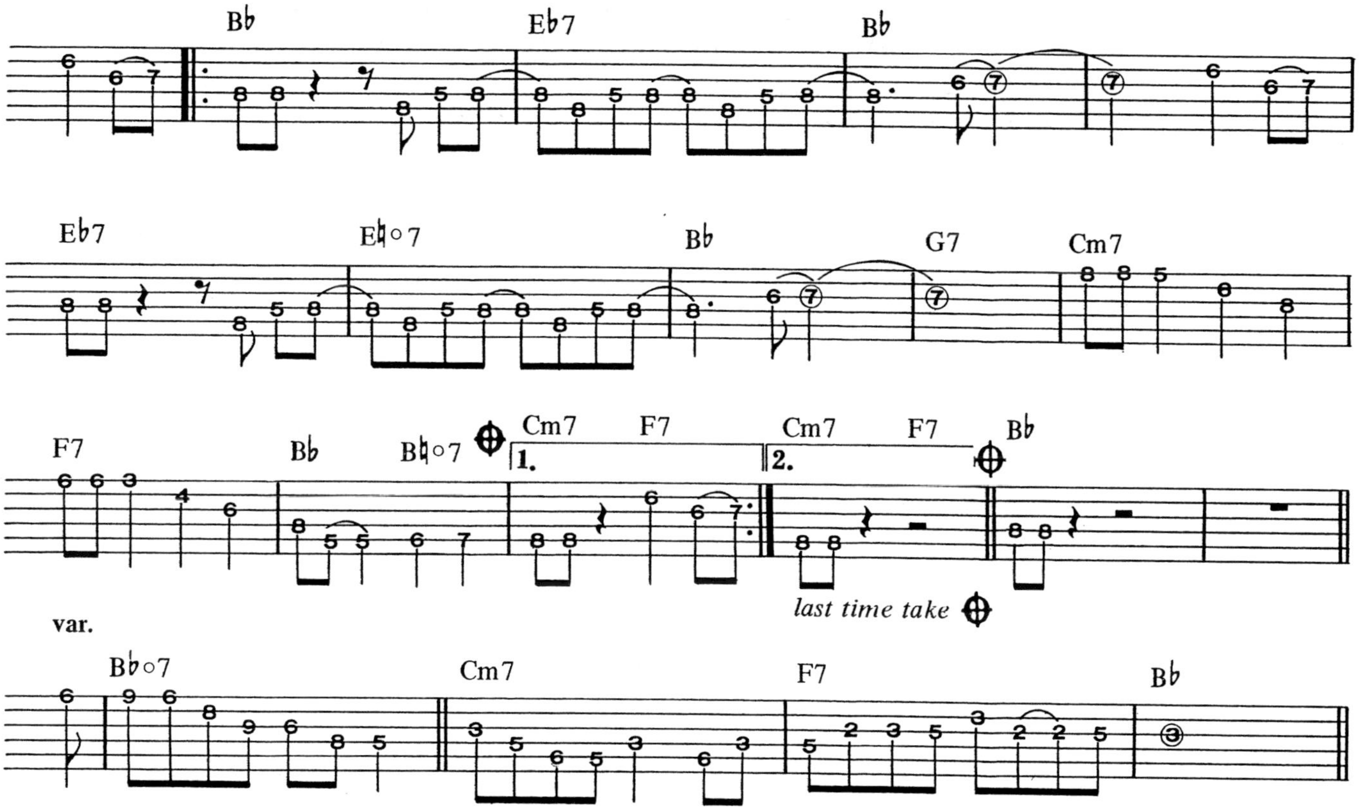

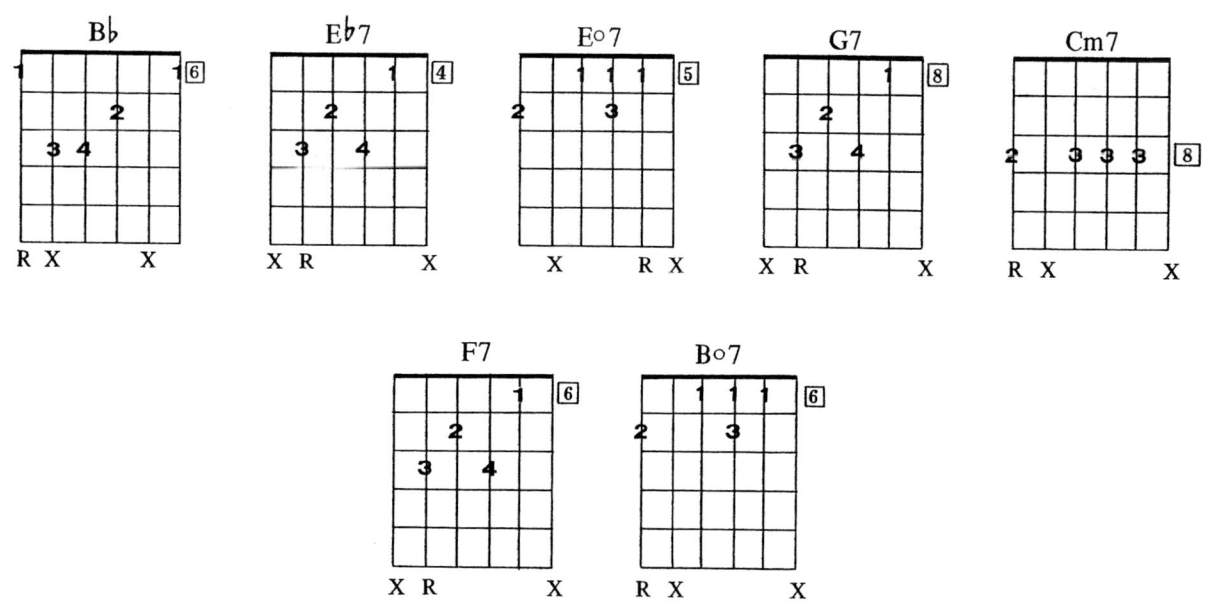

© Copyright 1990 by Dix Bruce.

Fast Blues
Mandolin Tablature

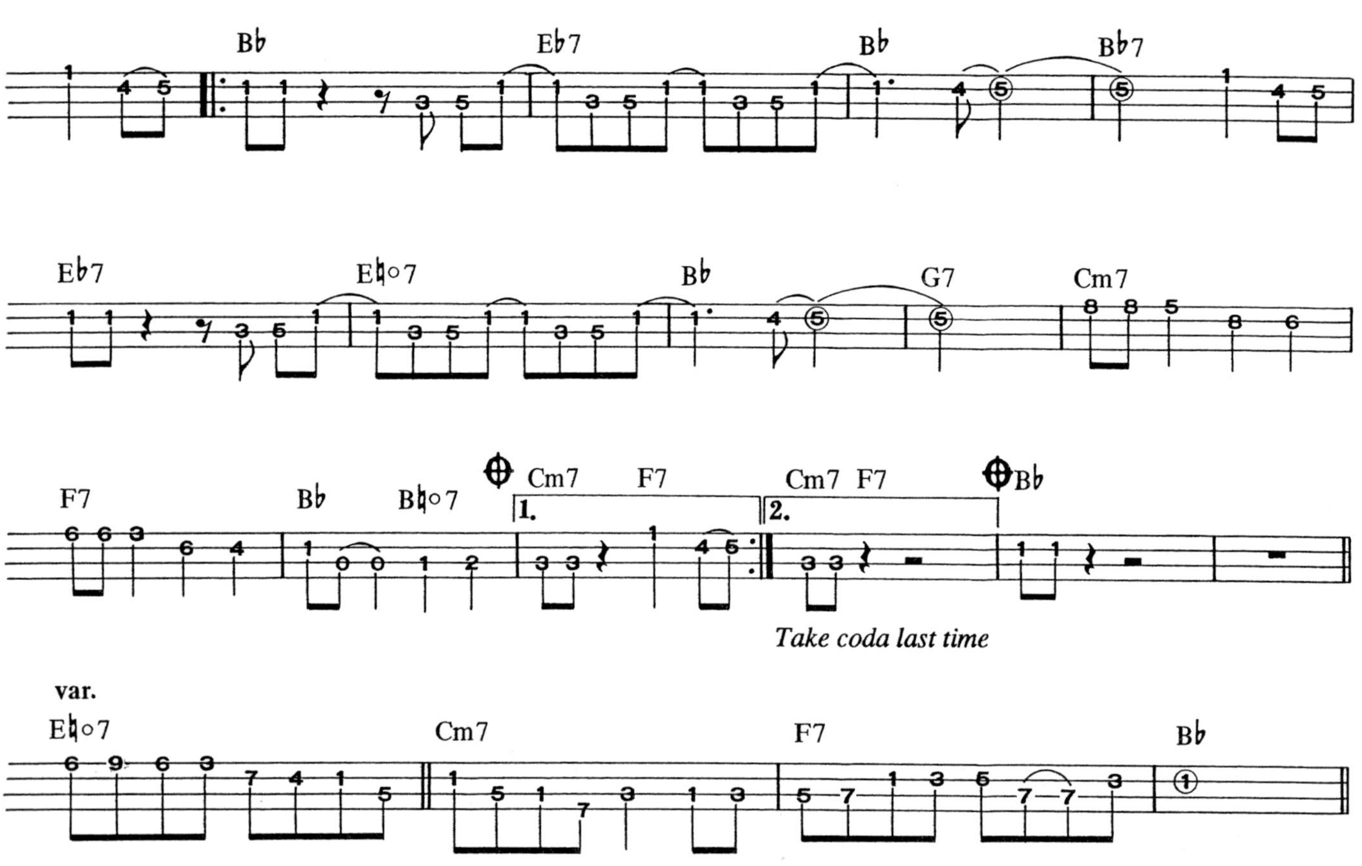

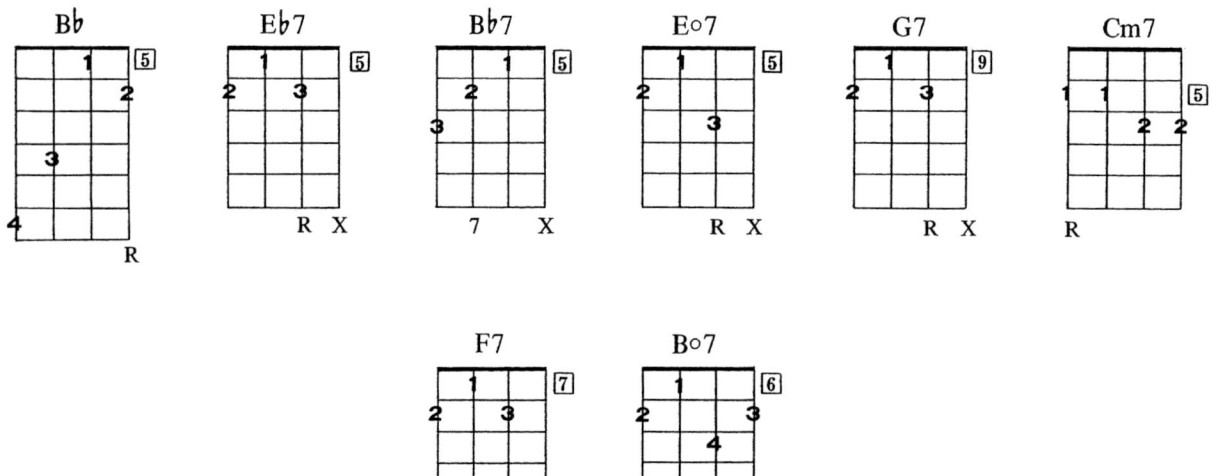

© Copyright 1990 by Dix Bruce.

GAL BE BAD

Most of the moves in this tune should already be familiar to you. The secret to it lies in making the changes flow. It's similar to "Lady Be Good." Notice the slightly different turnaround in measure 7. Try substituting a I-vi-ii-V progression in the last 2 measures. How about a iii-VI-ii-V? Again, this is an AABA-type tune.

Quotable quotes: "Jazz is hard to pick" — Benny Martin. "Jazz is never playing the same thing once" — unknown. Key of G.

Gal Be Bad
C Instruments

© Copyright 1990 by Dix Bruce.

Gal Be Bad
Guitar Tablature

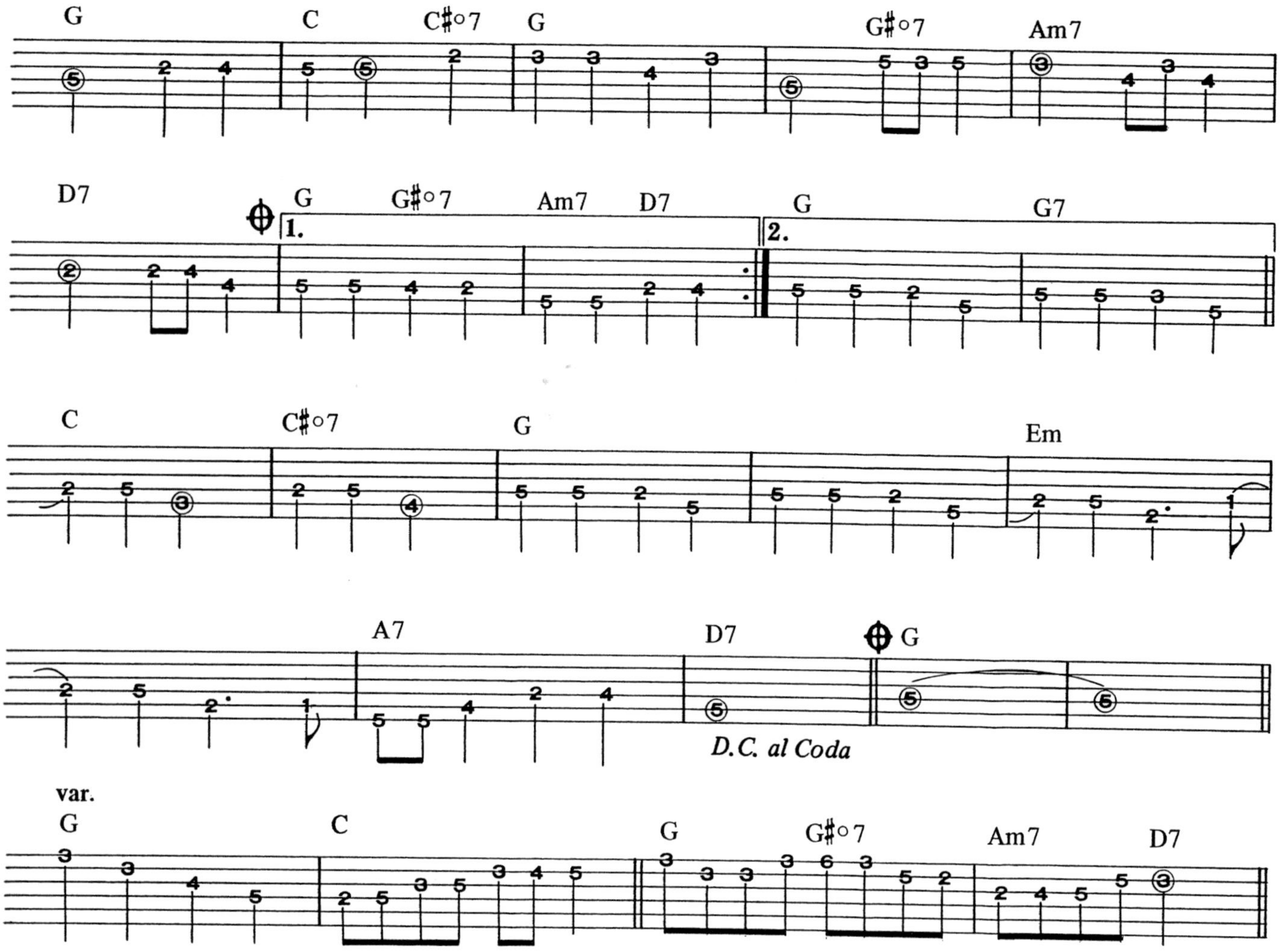

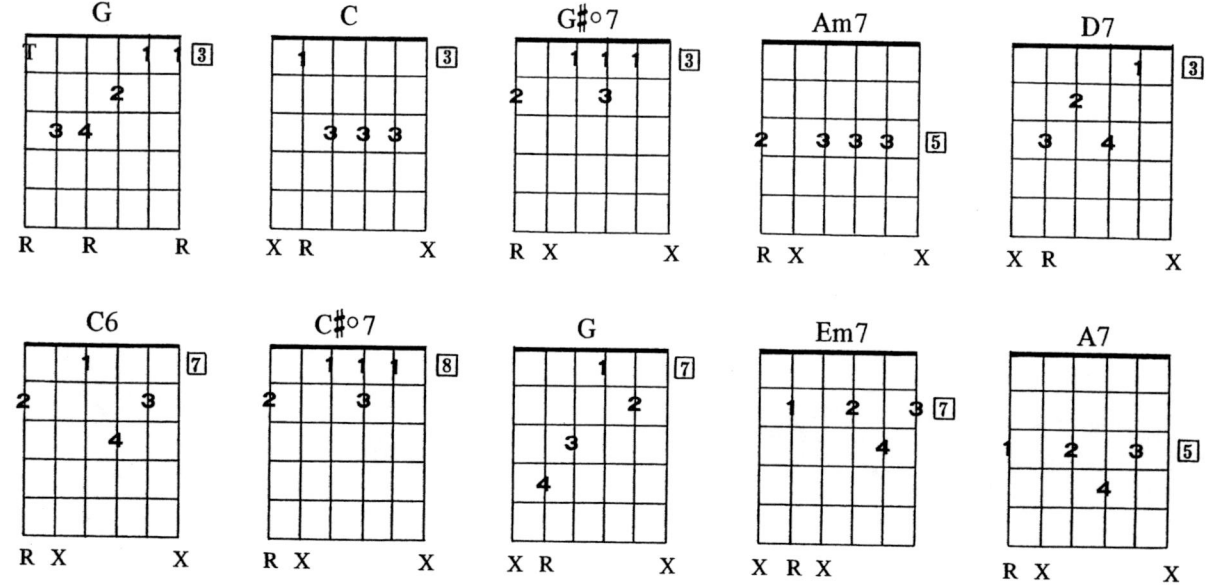

© Copyright 1990 by Dix Bruce.

Gal Be Bad
Mandolin Tablature

© Copyright 1990 by Dix Bruce.

BLUES IN C MINOR

When you get into the blues, don't forget about minor keys. Be sure to play the rhythm hits on the melody in measures 3, 7, and 11. Note the slightly simpler changes on the solo section. This progression will work with the melody to John Coltrane's "Mr. PC." Coltrane was so hip that he named the tune for the personal computer years before anyone else sensed its importance in the 1980s.

In the introduction to this book, I mentioned the importance of listening to and studying other players. To do this you need to transcribe licks or solos from records and tapes. If you've tried it, you know how difficult and frustrating this can be. The playing goes by awfully fast, isn't repeated, and may not be tuned to standard A-440. The solution is to spend a couple hundred dollars to buy a two-speed tape recorder with pitch control. These cassette machines play and record at the regular cassette speed and at one-half speed. The half-speed option slows anything down to, you guessed it, one-half speed, one octave lower than at normal speed. Most have sophisticated cue and review functions so that you can zero in on one or two notes. The pitch control allows you to tune the tape to your instrument. They're a wonderful tool for transcription. Key of Cm.

Minor Blues

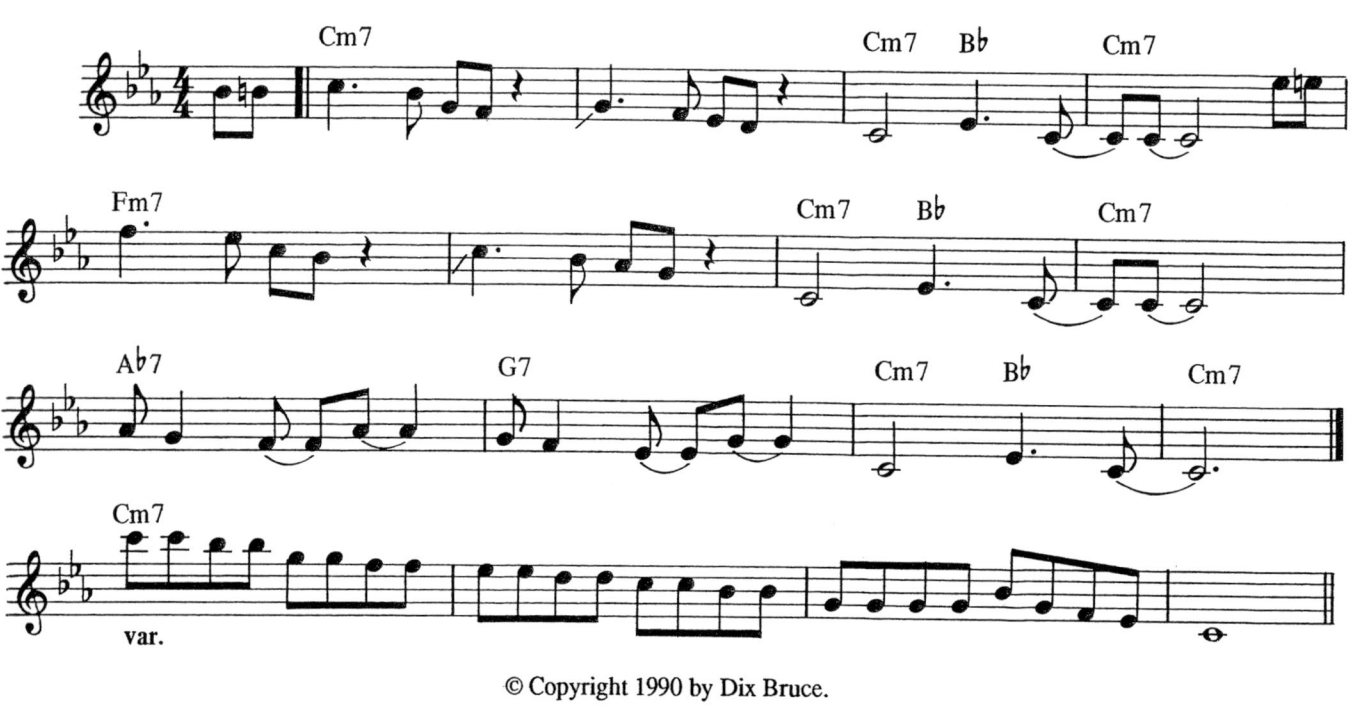

© Copyright 1990 by Dix Bruce.

C Minor Blues
Guitar Tablature

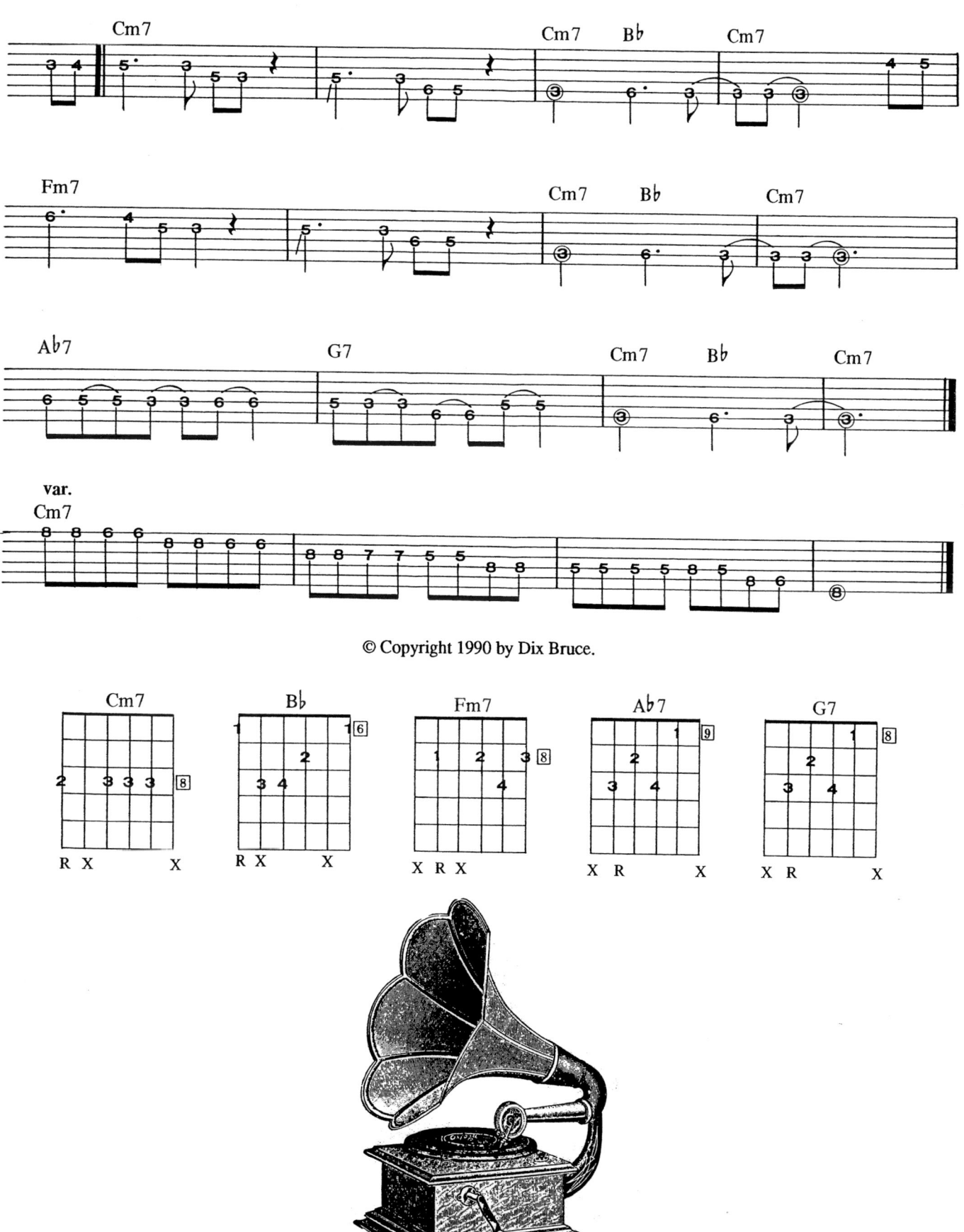

© Copyright 1990 by Dix Bruce.

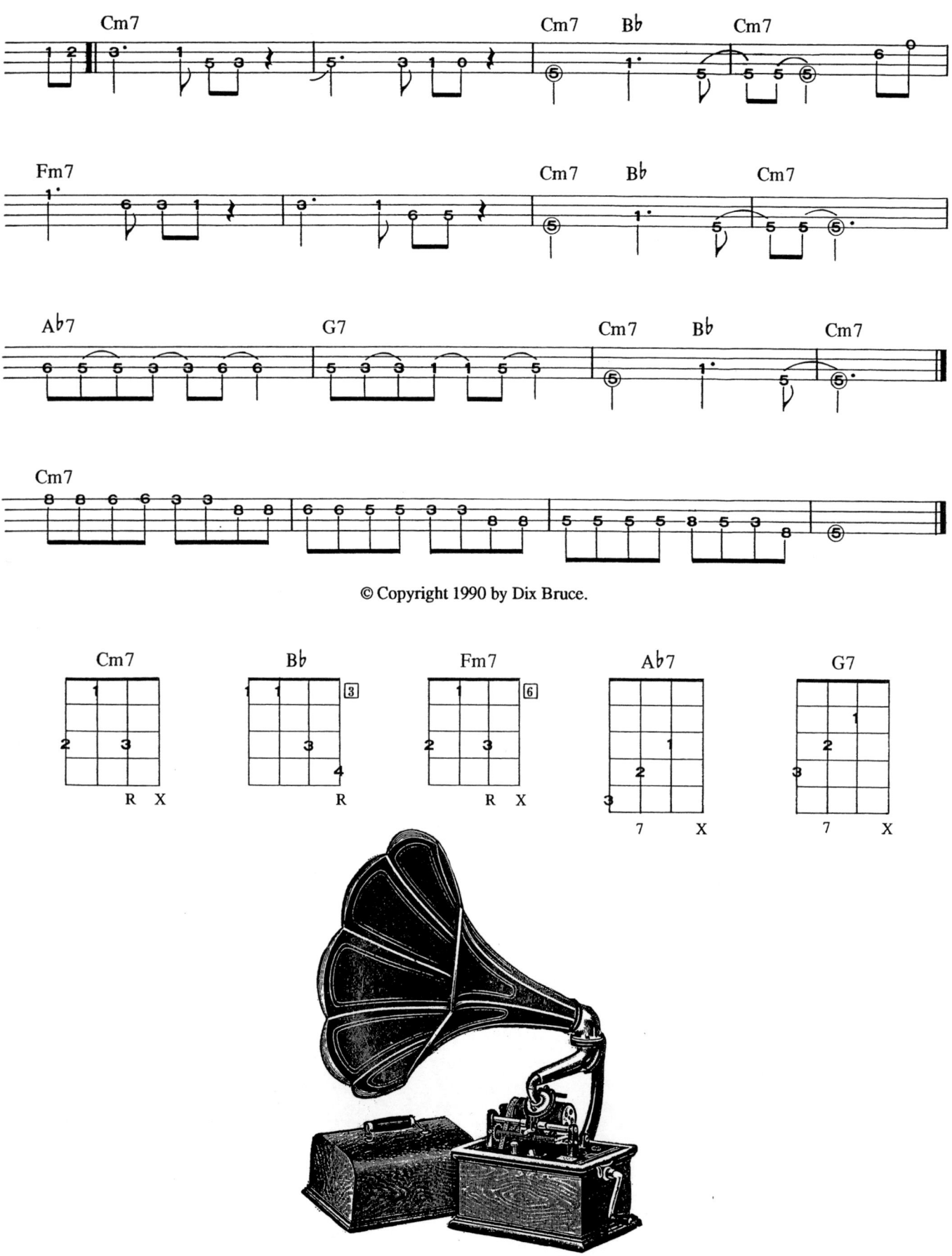

SOLO THE SUN

This progression is another of the biggies. The descending-key scheme with its various ii-V-I passages can be found in tunes like "How High the Moon," "Ornithology," and my own "Bright Angel" (published in *Mandolin World News,* Vol. VII #3). "Solo the Sun" starts in the key of G and moves through F, E♭, and Gm. It's great for working on your ii-V-I licks and especially good practice to transpose one lick through all the different keys.

In the 10th measure you have a ii-V change that resolves to a one *minor* chord. You'll need to change your lick accordingly here by flatting any third that is played over the minor one chord. You also notice that the ii has been modified with a "flat five" and the V with a "flat nine" (an E♭ instead of the E natural). Both of these changes are typical, and often an option, when moving to a minor one chord. In this case we really have to play the Am7♭5 since we have an E♭ melody note. By the way, m7♭5 chords are also called "half diminished" chords.

The 15th bar shows another common turnaround, basically a substituted iii-VI-ii-V, with a B♭7 in place of the expected E7. This is known as the "flat five" substitution. (The five of E is B, flat the B and you get B♭. For a D7 the substitution would be A♭7.) Try this turnaround in the other tunes and in other keys. Key of G.

Solo the Sun
C Instruments

© Copyright 1990 by Dix Bruce.

Solo the Sun
Guitar Tablature

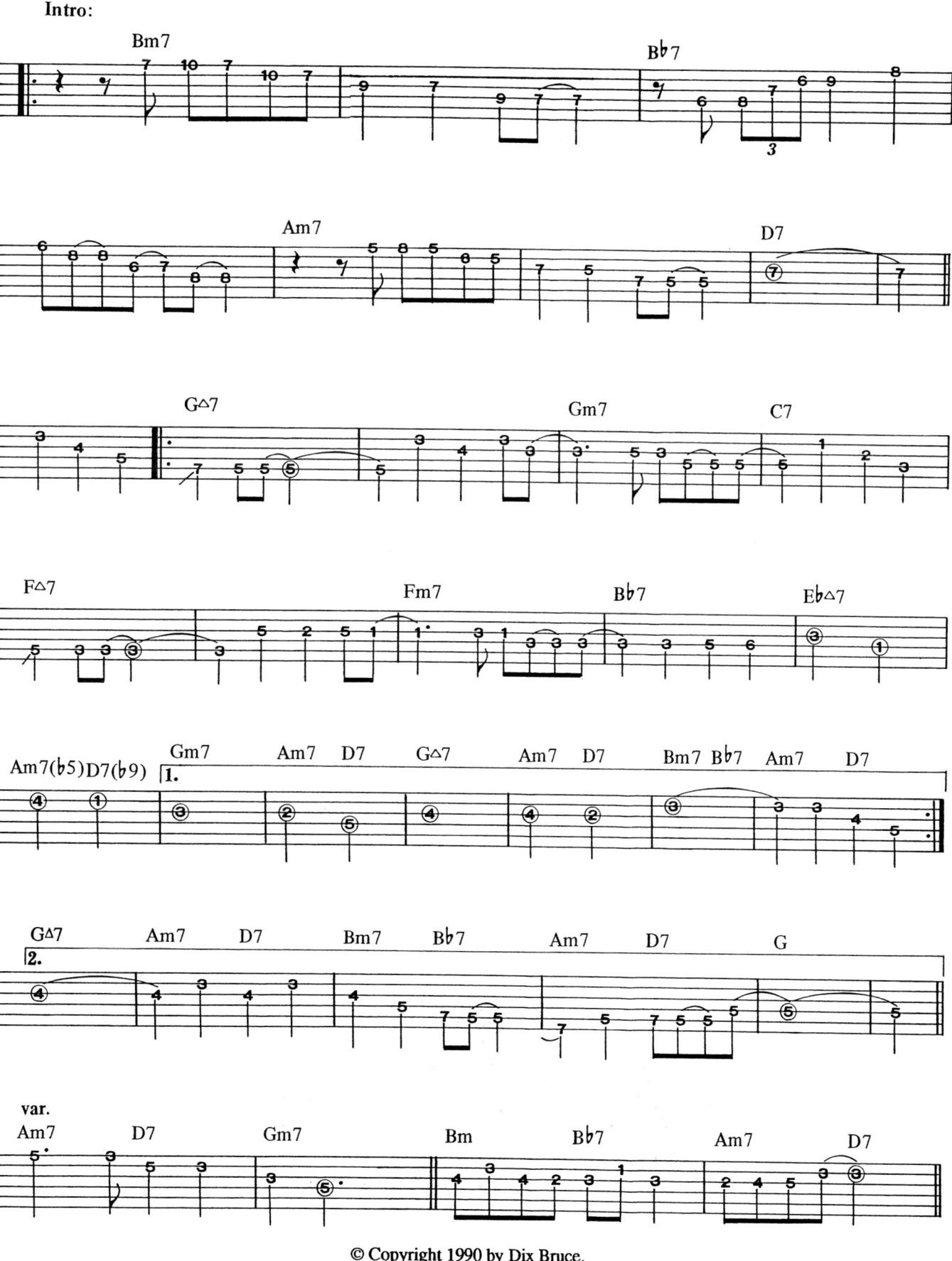

© Copyright 1990 by Dix Bruce.

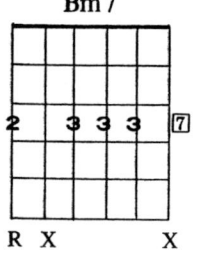 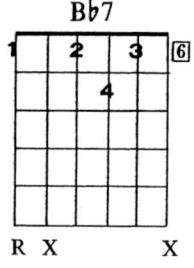 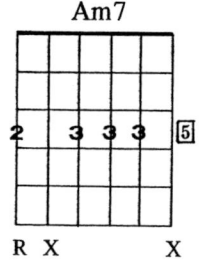 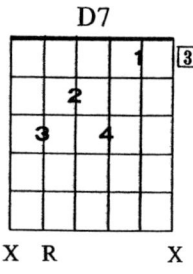
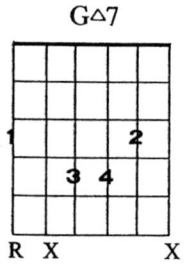 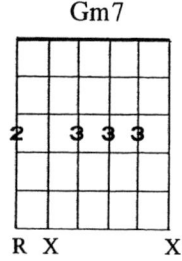 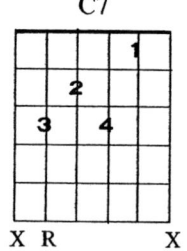 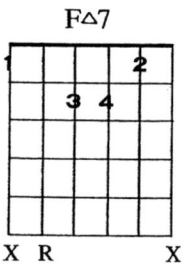
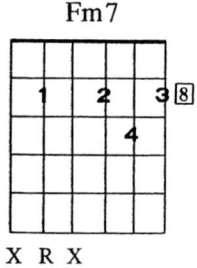 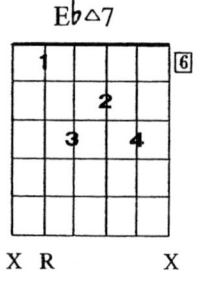 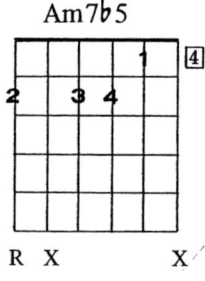
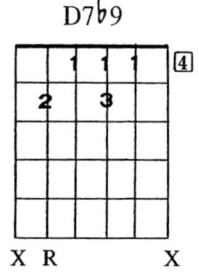 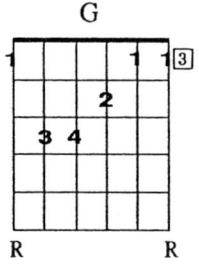

Solo the Sun
Mandolin Tablature

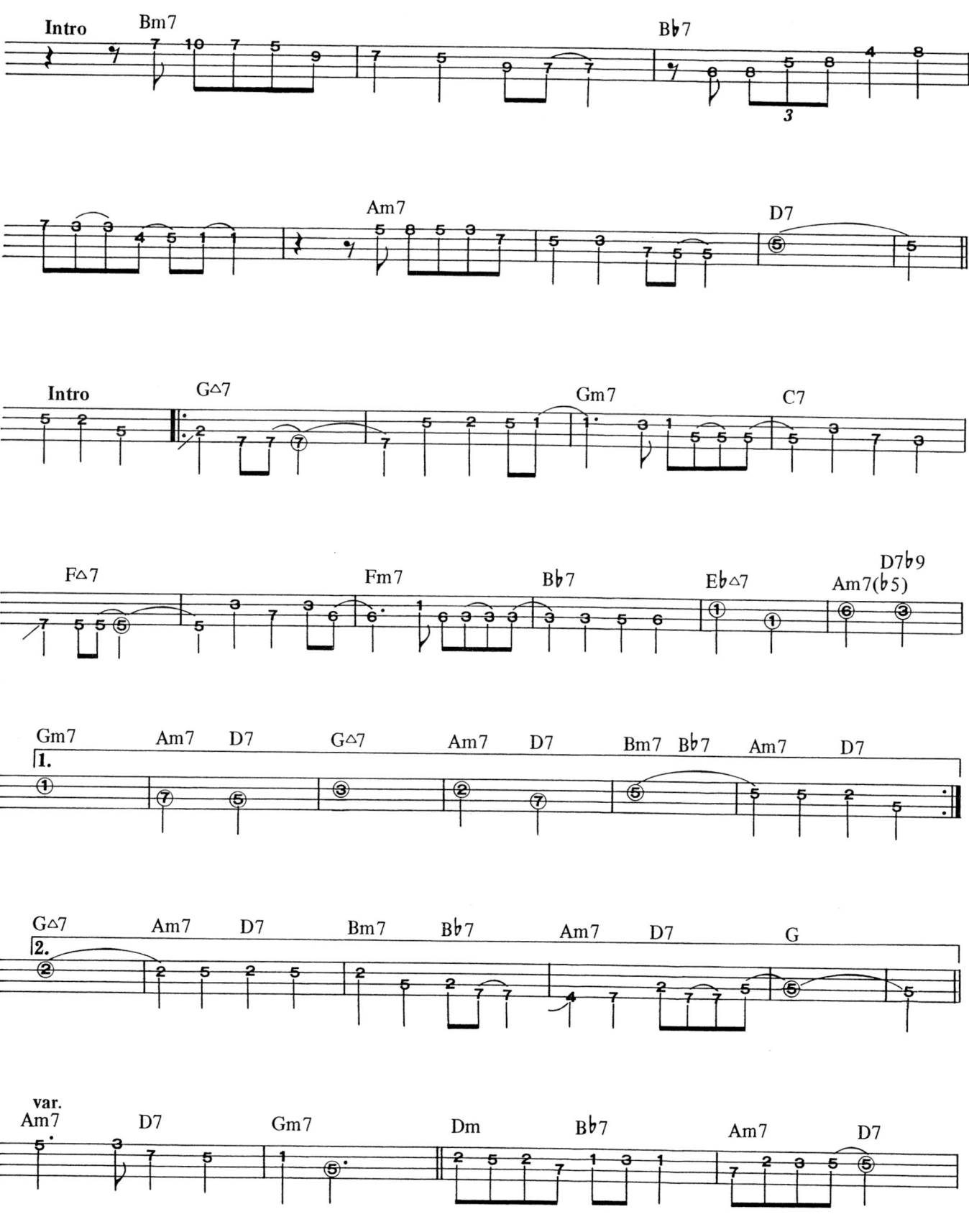

© Copyright 1990 by Dix Bruce.

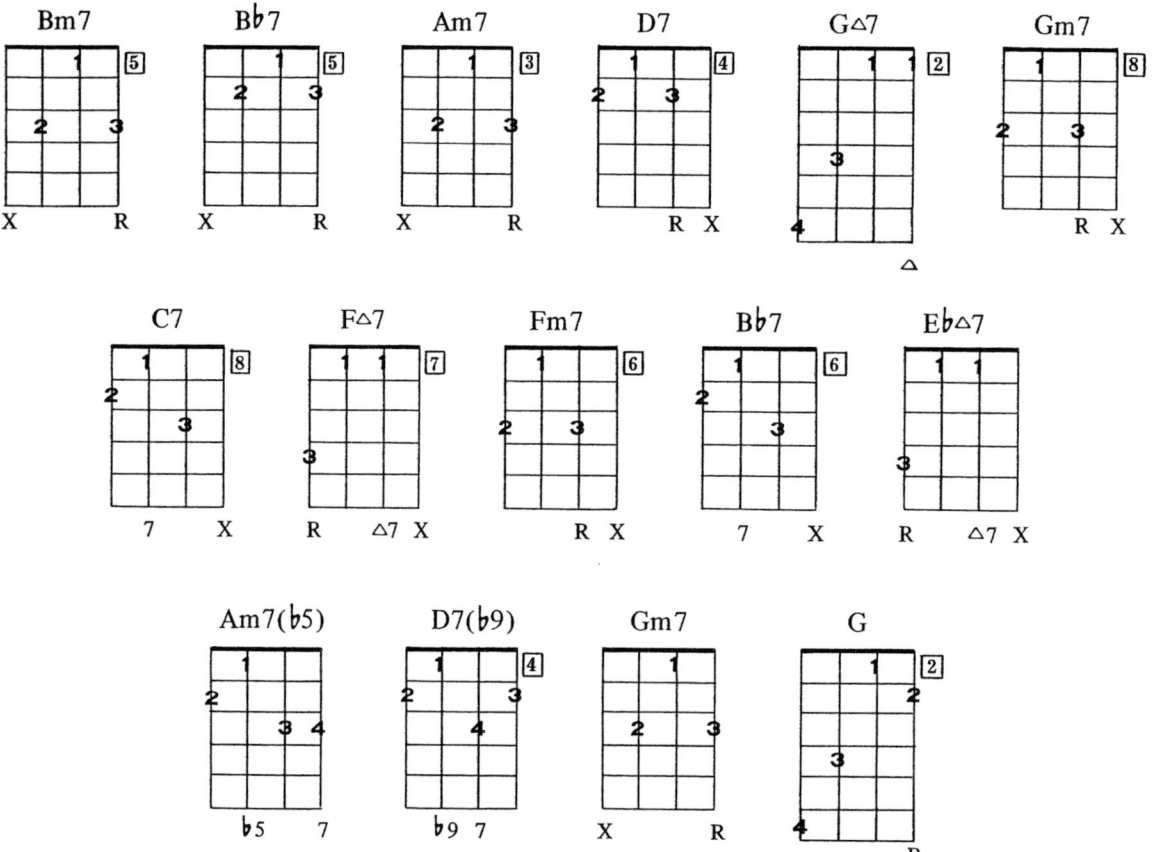

6/8 BLUES

6/8 time is not found quite as often as 4/4 or 2/4 in jazz, but it is another time signature that you should be able to play in. Note the descending bass line beginning in the 9th measure. Key of Gm.

Minor Blues Waltz

© Copyright 1990 by Dix Bruce.

Minor Blues Waltz
Guitar Tablature

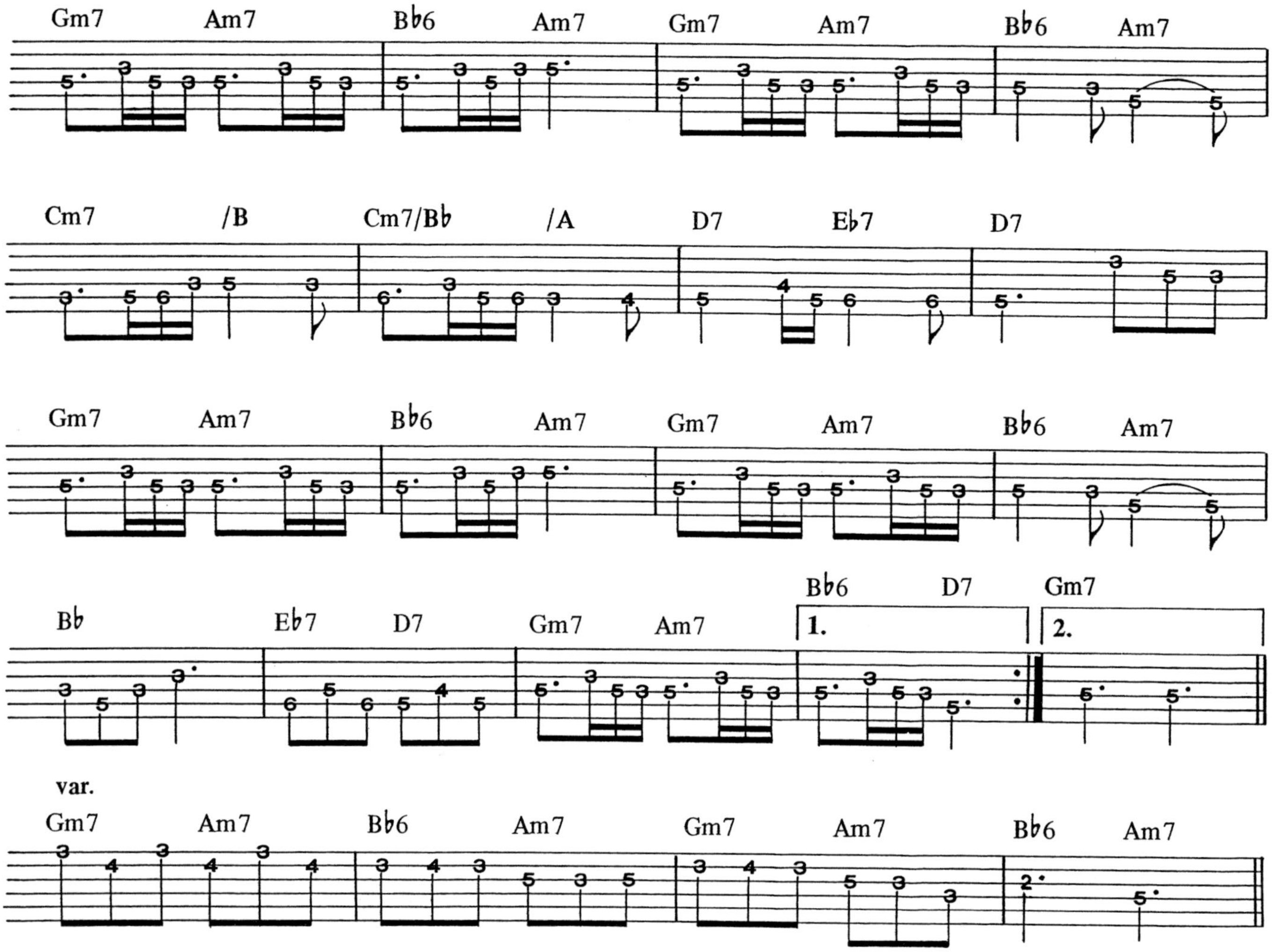

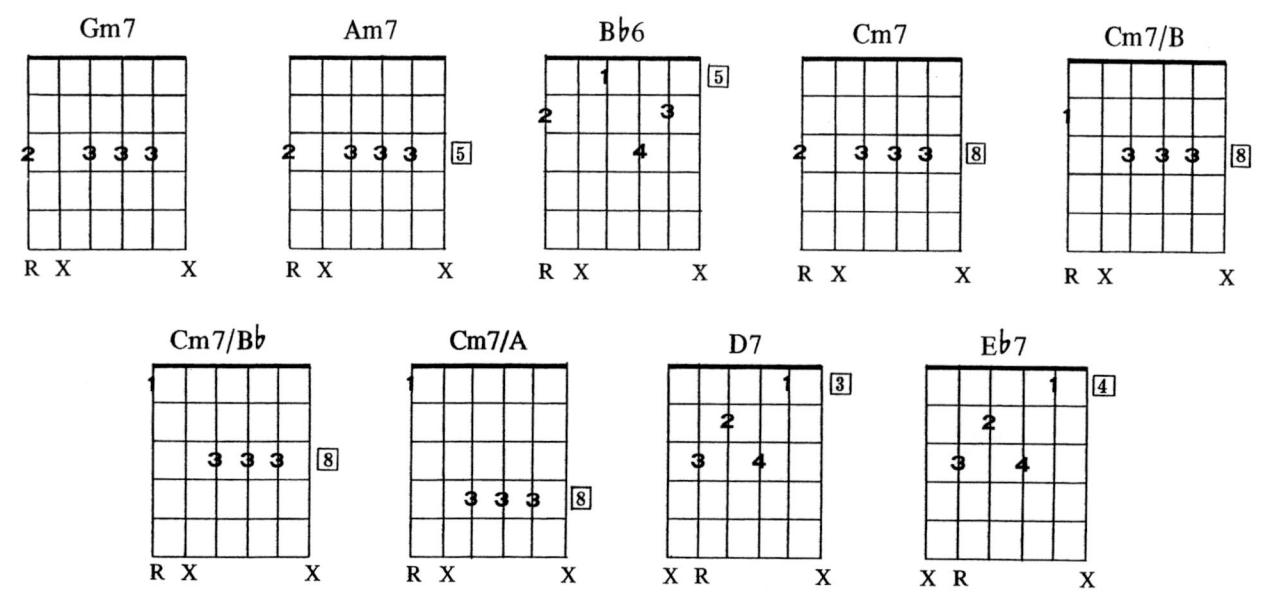

© Copyright 1990 by Dix Bruce.

Minor Blues Waltz
Mandolin Tablature

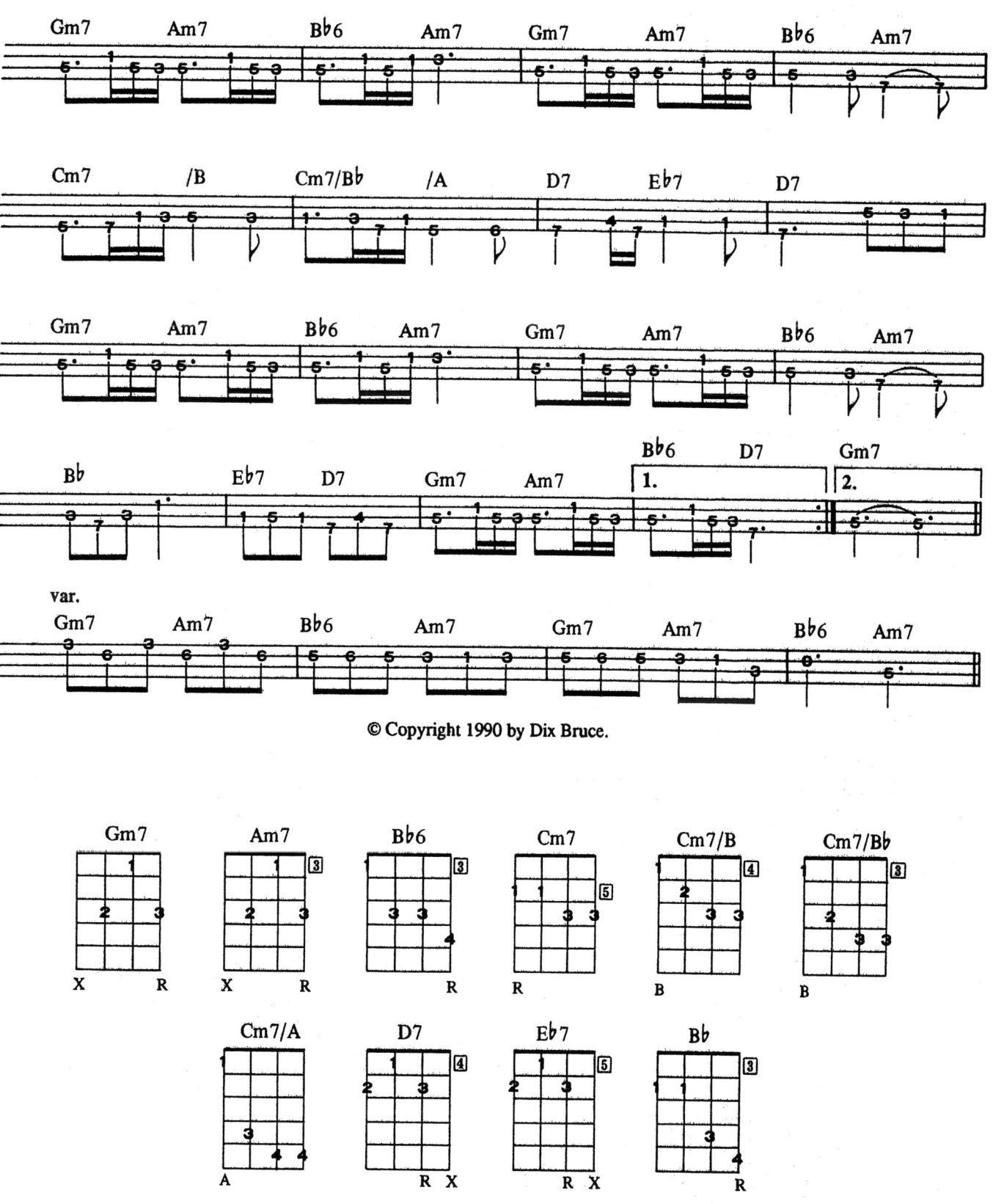

© Copyright 1990 by Dix Bruce.

YELLOWSTONE

"Yellowstone" is similar to tunes like the old chestnuts "In a Mellow Tone" and "Rose Room." The key, A♭, may throw you at first, but try to look at individual dominant chords and 2- and 4-measure passages as building blocks to the whole. Break it down and figure out licks to the parts. Fit the parts together smoothly and you'll be sailing. Key of A♭.

© Copyright 1990 by Dix Bruce.

Yellowstone
Guitar Tablature

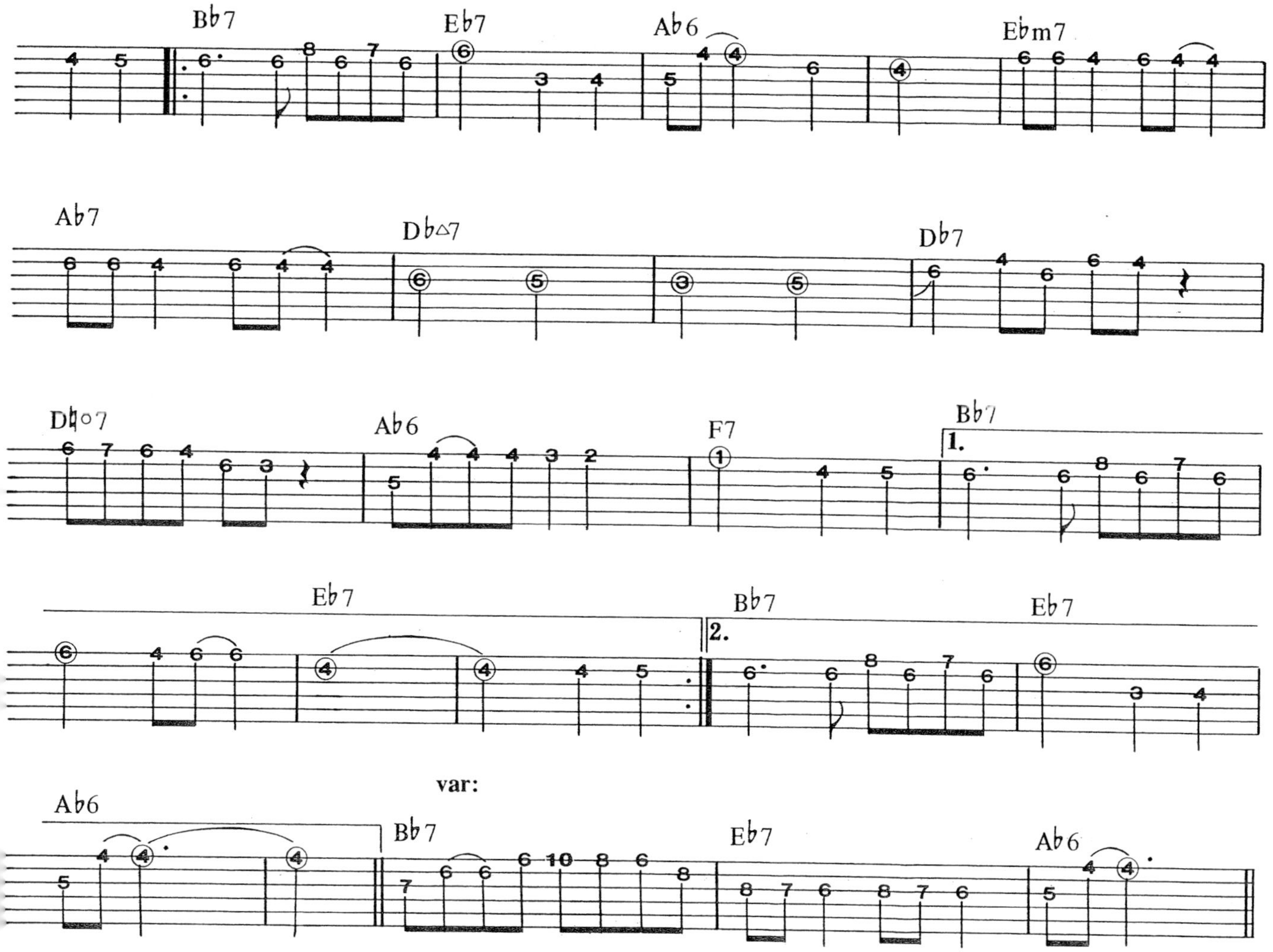

© Copyright 1990 by Dix Bruce.

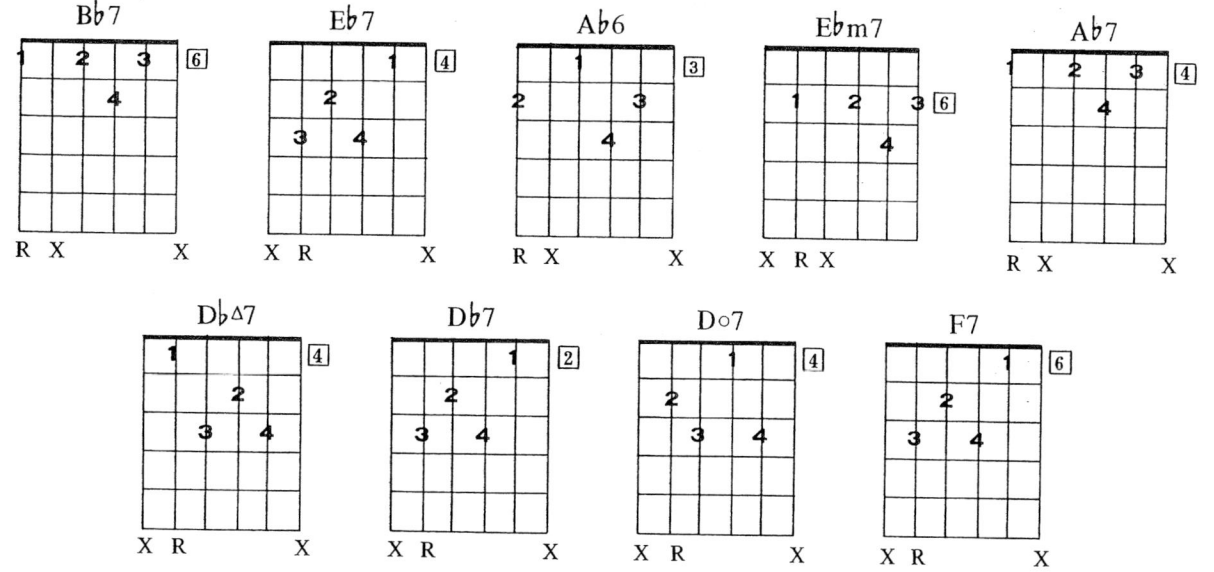

Yellowstone
Mandolin Tablature

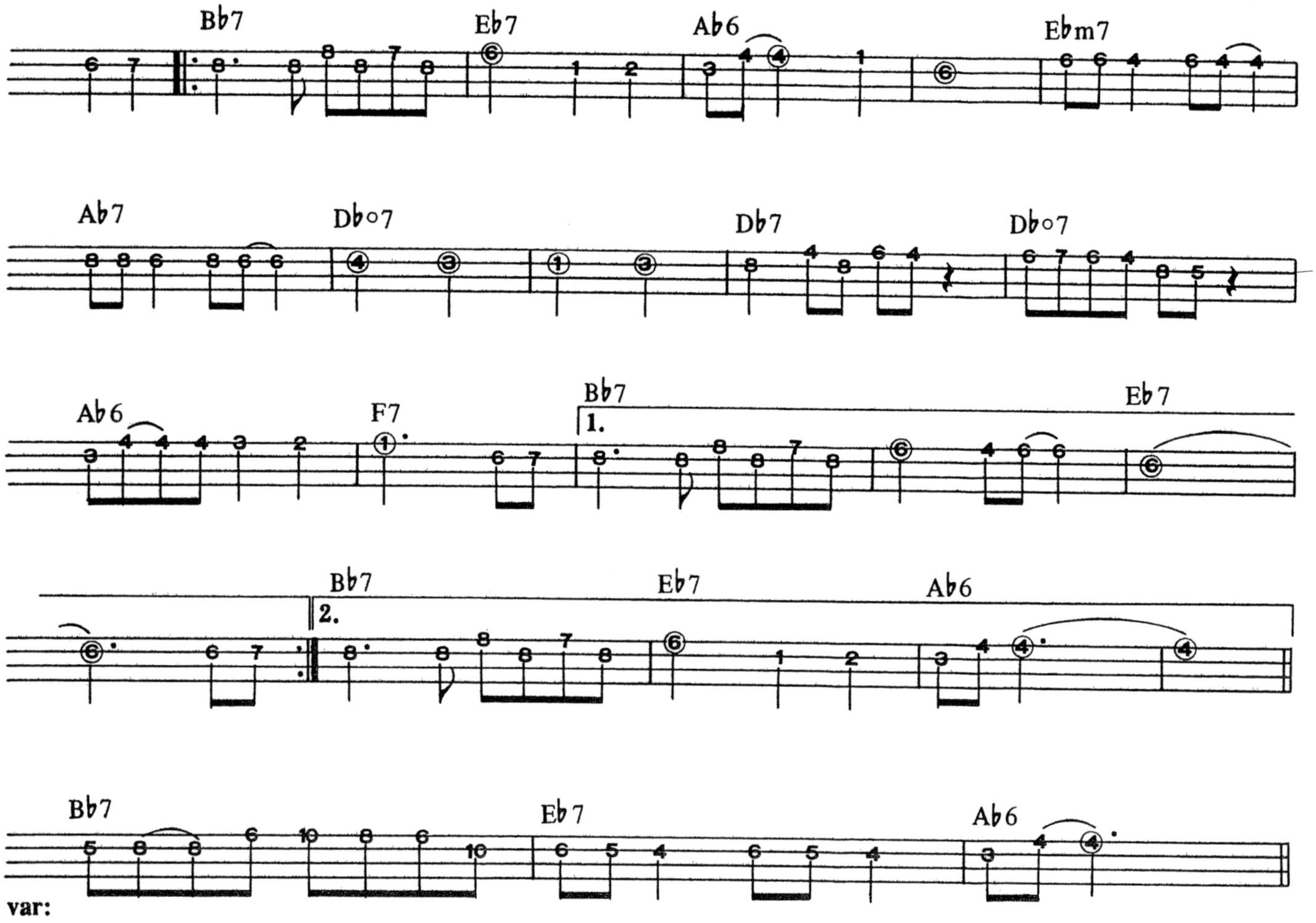

© Copyright 1990 by Dix Bruce.

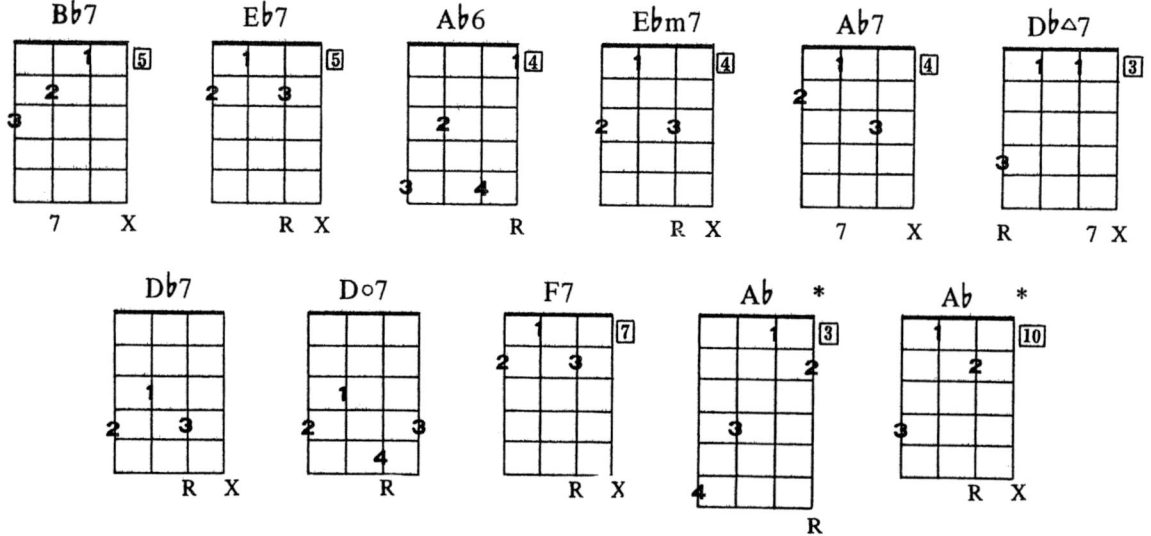

*Can be used as substitute for the A♭6 chord.

DISCOGRAPHY

None of the etudes in this book are currently available on record. However, the chord changes are found everywhere in the jazz repertoire. Many of the similar tunes have been recorded on thousands of great records. Browsing through the jazz record bins, checking artists and song titles, is your best bet to tracking them down. The list below mentions just a few of the swing & jazz greats you should check out.

Cannonball Adderly	Earl Hines	Sonny Rollins	Louis Armstrong
Billie Holliday	Jimmy Rushing	George Barnes	Harry James
Pharoah Sanders	Count Basie	Jazz at the Philharmonic	Shakti
Sidney Bechet	Artie Shaw	Bix Beiderbecke	James P. Johnson
Archie Shepp	George Benson	Thad Jones	George Shearing
Art Blakey	Louis Jordan	Wayne Shorter	Clifford Brown
Stan Kenton	Horace Silver	Ray Brown	Barney Kessell
Zoot Sims	Dave Brubeck	Rahsaan Roland Kirk	Frank Sinatra
Jethro Burns	Lee Konitz	Stuff Smith	Kenny Burrell
Eddie Lang	Spyrogyra	Benny Carter	Jimmy Lunceford
Sonny Stitt	Ray Charles	John McLaughlin	Buddy Tate
Don Cherry	Marian McPartland	Art Tatum	Charlie Christian
Shelley Manne	Cecil Taylor	Kenny Clarke	Johnny Mercer
Jack Teagarden	Nat Cole	Clarles Mingus	Clark Terry
Ornette Coleman	Modern Jazz Quartet	Mel Torme	John Coltrane
Thelonious Monk	McCoy Tyner	Tadd Dameron	Wes Montgomery
Sarah Vaughn	Miles Davis	Jelly Roll Morton	Joe Venuti
Eric Dolphy	Bennie Moten	Fats Waller	Tommy & Jimmy Dorsey
Gerry Mulligan	Dinah Washington	Roy Eldridge	Fats Navarro
Weather Report	Duke Ellington	Red Nichols	Chick Webb

Bill Evans	Red Norvo	Ben Webster	Ella Fitzgerald
King Oliver	Paul Whiteman	Stan Getz	Kid Ory
Teddy Wilson	Dizzy Gillispie	Charlie Parker	Jimmy Witherspoon
Benny Goodman	Art Pepper	Lester Young	Dexter Gordon
Oscar Peterson	Joe Zawinul	Stephane Grappelli	Bud Powell
David Grisman	Quintette of the Hot Club of France	Lionel Hampton	Herbie Hancock
Don Redman	Coleman Hawkins	Django Reinhardt	Fletcher Henderson
Buddy Rich	Woody Herman	Max Roach	

BIBLIOGRAPHY

There are literally *hundreds* of good swing & jazz books on the market; histories, theory books, books on how to improvise, lists of the greatest recordings and/or players, biographies, books that deal with jazz on your specific instrument, collections of recorded solos, and more. I couldn't begin to highlight all the useful texts. Libraries, and of course music stores, will have good selections. Here are a very few from my bookshelf. You may find the collections of recorded solos (*) to be very useful in composing your own solos. Check *Downbeat* magazine for news of the latest jazz books.

The Illustrated Encyclopedia of Jazz (Harmony Books)
The Jazz Idiom by Jerry Coker (Spectrum)
Improvising Jazz by Jerry Coker (Spectrum)
Patterns for Jazz by Jerry Coker (Studio Publications)
Charlie Parker Omnibook–Transcribed Solos (Atlantic)*
Jazz Masters Series: Benny Goodman, Miles Davis, Django Reinhardt, Thelonious Monk, and others (Music Sales Corp.)*

Also by Dix Bruce:

BackUp Trax: Old Time & Fiddle Tunes. (Mel Bay). Learn melodies and practice soloing on 14 of the most popular old-time and fiddle tunes such as "Temperance Reel," "Sally Goodin," "Blackberry Blossom," and more! Play along with a great string-band rhythm section. The recording has all of the tunes at slow and regular speeds and allows you to hear just rhythm, just lead, or both! You supply the lead. We'll play all night long!

BackUp Trax: Basic Blues for Guitar Booklet/CD set (Mel Bay). Learn to play 14 classic blues the best way -- by doing! This booklet and CD provide your backup band as you explore Country and Urban, Acoustic and Electric, Delta, Texas, Chicago, Slide Guitar, Alternate Tuning, Traditional, and Modern styles in many different major and minor keys and in a variety of tempos. Beginners and intermediate players can practice basic skills. Advanced players can hone their improvisation chops. The split track recording allows you to hear either just the melody from one speaker, just the rhythm section from the other, or both for maximum flexibility and specific study. The booklet includes melodies, chord diagrams and guitar tablature.

BackUp Trax: Old Time & Fiddle Tunes for Cello Booklet/CD set (Mel Bay). Learn melodies and practice soloing on fourteen of the most popular old time and fiddle tunes. Play along with a great string band rhythm section: guitar, mandolin, and string bass. The CD has all of the tunes at slow and regular speeds with melodies, and allows you to hear just rhythm, just lead, or both. Great for cello, string bass, bass guitar, or any bass clef instrument.

First Lessons Mandolin Book/CD set (Mel Bay) First Lessons Mandolin teaches the absolute basics of learning to play mandolin from holding the pick to performing easy mandolin tunes. It doesn't get any easier the this! Students learn how to hold the mandolin correctly, how to read mandolin tablature, basic note reading, the most popular mandolin chords, how to play easy melodies in several musical styles, basic picking technique, how to tune the mandolin, and much more. Along the way students will learn about the greatest mandolin players and their music.

You Can Teach Yourself® Country Guitar Book/CD set (Mel Bay) This is a step-at-a-time enjoyable method for learning to play great sounding country guitar, Dix Bruce, in his humorous yet musically "right-on" teaching style, introduces you to country back-up, bass runs, Carter-style bluegrass picking, the Nashville Numbering System for indicating chord changes, use of the capo, transposition, and much more. Work at your own pace and learn to sound like the country greats! Written in standard notation and tablature.

You Can Teach Yourself® Mandolin Book/CD set (Mel Bay) Another great "Teach Yourself" book with "play-along" examples to help you get started. You'll learn all about accompanying yourself and others, common chords and useful strums, reading simple melodies, playing a colorful assortment of mandolin folk songs, and much more. In notation and tablature. The CD is in split-track format and features each song played at both slow and normal tempos!

For information, write: Dix Bruce, c/o Musix, P.O. Box 231005, Pleasant Hill, CA 94523.